JOBS
AND
COVID-19

ALSO BY NARINDER MEHTA

How to Get the Job You Want and Build a Great Career:
A Manual for College Students and Young Professionals (2009)

Five Steps to Your Next Job:
A Powerful Manual for Job Search and Career Development (2011)

Ace Your Job Search in 5 Steps:
Powerful Techniques for Building a Successful Career (2016)

JOBS
AND
COVID-19

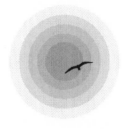

THE PATHWAY TO A
HAPPY CAREER

NARINDER
MEHTA

First Published, 2021

ISBN: 9798648910621
Independently published

Library of Congress Control Number: 2021908701

Published by Mehta Consulting, PO Box 547, Dover, MA 02030-0547

Printed in the United States of America

Cover design by Berge Design

For

Sampath, Ravi, Tiffany,

Arden, and Vivien

CONTENTS

FOREWORD

A re you looking for a new job because you were laid off or
furloughed during Covid-19? Are you looking to change
jobs for a better career opportunity? Are you looking for your
first job after graduation? Are you looking for some tried
and true tips for achieving long-term career success? If you
answered yes, then this is the right book for you!

This book is a must read for anyone interested in securing
a good job and achieving long-term career success. It is a book
you should not refer to just once, but time and time again. It is
packed with inspiration and information that will help you to
position yourself for your best career future. It is inspiring and
well-written.

I am a professor who has studied the topic of job search
and unemployment for over 30 years. I have interacted with
many job search counselors and looked at many job search
books. I feel well-suited to say that this book will be helpful to
you! The author of this book speaks straight from the heart.
He shares many lessons he has learned in his impressive career.
These lessons will be of enormous value to you in building a
framework for success for your life-long career.

This book will help you build a career well matched with
your skills. Each person is unique with a different set of skills,
traits, and job interests. What is a great job for one person will
not suit someone else. The first step to achieve a successful and
happy career is to identify the top skills you enjoy using and
then target your efforts at jobs that match your skills. Many
people go through life unhappy at work because they end up
in jobs that do not fit their skills or job interests. The book will

help you to identify the skills you enjoy using and give you guidance to get the jobs that match your skills.

This valuable resource for job search and career development covers the essential steps: matching your skills to jobs; preparing online profiles and resumes; connecting with potential employers; interviewing for jobs; and negotiating salary and benefits. The book includes guidance for using the Internet and provides links to some of the best available websites for career information. The book also includes a chapter on how to develop a happy career and provides useful tips to achieve career success. The Appendix included in the book provides a framework for overcoming the roadblocks on the way to achieving successful results.

The book is based on the author's personal experiences as a successful business manager responsible for hiring employees for many companies, and as an executive recruiter who interacted with hiring managers of a variety of companies. He has extensively researched the impact of Covid-19 on jobs and shares a framework that will help people to prosper in the post-pandemic workplace.

Take this book to your favorite coffee shop, or sit outside if the weather is good, and enjoy, think, and plan! You must take control over your career to get where you want to go.

—Connie Wanberg, Ph.D., Professor and Industrial Relations Faculty Excellence Chair, Department of Work and Organizations, Carlson School of Management, University of Minnesota

INTRODUCTION

Covid-19 pandemic has forever changed the workplace and how we live. No one could have predicted what happened in 2020. It was the year in which we saw the greatest loss of life and livelihoods in the last one hundred years. While we saw immense suffering, we also saw the emergence of new technologies that will change how we live. We saw a rapid acceleration in e-commerce, automation and remote work.

The last time a pandemic hit with a comparable force was back in 1918. That pandemic, also known as the Spanish flu, was an influenza pandemic that killed 675,000 Americans out of a population of 106 million. It lasted for more than two years, from February 1918 to April 1920, and created four successive waves.

The pandemic of a century ago was followed by a boom known as the Roaring Twenties. It saw the adoption of the assembly line for automobile production, introduction of the radio and motion pictures as well as many electrical appliances. It improved the quality of life for average American through the availability of automobiles, refrigerators, washing machines and other appliances. The rise in the automobile usage led to investments in roads and suburbs and resulted in higher standards of living.

As we move through the current pandemic, we need to ask whether the history will repeat itself. **Are we going to see the 2020s roar with the same vigor and speed as did the 1920s?** That is quite possible! We have seen some amazing transformations during the first year of the coronavirus pandemic. We have never seen remote working spread like this. We saw home delivery of goods as we never imagined. We saw telemedicine grow at a speed we never thought possible. We have seen many Covid-19 vaccines developed within months. That is a process which used to take many years in the past. We have seen the rapid development of video conferencing and cloud computing that will pay handsome dividends in the years ahead. We are seeing many innovations in artificial intelligence and robotics. Still it remains to be seen whether the 2020s economy will rise the way the 1920s economy did.

This book is intended to help people prosper during the pandemic and in the economy following the pandemic. Millions of jobs have been lost and will not come back. At the same time, millions of new jobs have emerged in digital commerce, telemedicine, automation and other sectors of the economy. These new jobs require different skills and the use of new job search techniques. This book will show a pathway to build a successful and happy career. It will show how to evaluate personal skills and experiences to match the new job requirements. The book explains the new job search techniques and shows how to make use of the vast resources available on the Internet.

We are on the road to recovery from the Covid-19 pandemic. There is light at the end of the tunnel, but there are still some hazards on the way. The process of restoring the economy and adding jobs in some industries will take several months, and perhaps many years. Yet, there are many employers who are looking for employees like you. As businesses increase operations, we will see growth and new career opportunities.

It is fortunate that vaccines have become available in such a short time. Vaccinations have begun all over the world and are becoming widely available. Economic activity is picking up as more people are vaccinated. Sustained recovery is on the way. The new job openings are on the rise in many sectors of the economy. We have recovered from some of the damage caused by the pandemic. The pandemic has created some fundamental shifts in the way we spend and how companies operate and some of these shifts are likely to be permanent.

The Covid-19 pandemic has changed the recruiting, interviewing, and hiring process. It has become remote from start to finish at many employers. Virtual hiring is new for many companies and they are navigating their way. For most job hunters, virtual interviewing is something they have not done before. It is new and different, and job seekers need to prepare for it.

I am writing this book to share with you the knowledge and experiences I have gained as a manager responsible for hiring employees for large as well as small companies, and as an executive recruiter who helped to find the management talent employers needed. I have also done extensive research to identify the latest trends, tools, and techniques for success in one's career.

The world around us is changing rapidly. While the traditional methods of job search such as sending resumes in response to job postings still work, they are much less reliable now. The Internet is continuing to evolve and change the way recruiting and interviewing is done. The job search process has radically changed during the pandemic. More and more employers as well as job hunters are using LinkedIn, Facebook, Twitter and other social media websites. The effective use of technology and the ability for virtual interviewing have become essential requirements to succeed in today's job market.

It is becoming harder to find the right job. Employers are willing to keep positions open for longer periods in expectation of finding the right employees with the needed skills. It used to take a few weeks to find a good job, and now it can take several months and sometimes more than a year. The number of long-term unemployed has grown and many able workers have dropped out of the work force.

Keep in mind that there are millions of job openings in the United States at any given time. These job openings arise from new business formations, expansion in companies, retirements, deaths, company mergers, relocations, and the emergence of new technologies. There is plenty of opportunity for those who have goals and the determination to turn those goals into reality.

What you need to succeed in today's job market is a clear picture of your dream job and what steps you need to take to get that job. Some people remain unemployed in the best of times, and there are others who find good jobs in very tough times.

As I look back upon my most memorable experiences, they were the result of dreaming about the things I wanted to achieve. At the time I had those thoughts, my dreams seemed impossible to accomplish. When I thought more about those dreams and how to turn them into reality, they came within reach. The distance between a dream and reality becomes short when you start to focus on how you are going to accomplish what you want. J. P. Morgan, the great industrialist, once said: "Go as far as you can see; when you get there, you will be able to see farther".

I am going to share with you some of the techniques I have used to achieve what I desired. There are many more ways that have been used by others to get what they wanted. I want to encourage you to reach for and accomplish whatever your heart desires, and learn from everyone around. Grasp whatever knowledge and ideas are available. Do not look for shortcomings in others, but look for areas of strength you can cultivate.

A job search is a sales campaign. I know something about selling having started as a sales trainee with American Express and then rising to the position of National Sales Director of the American Express Gold Card. I was then promoted to head up the national sales organization for the American Express Corporate Card. That journey in a sales management career enabled me to work with some of the best sales talent. I learned a lot over the years observing how these sales professionals achieved their goals.

You need a clear vision of your destination before you can get there. To find your dream job, you need to clearly define that job and lay out the path to get it. Some people know their dream jobs instinctively. They have a clear vision in their minds of what they want, develop plans to get there, and they reach their destinations. Others make efforts of varying degrees to identify the jobs they want. Some do extensive research of career descriptions to find what they want, some take career aptitude tests, some try to mirror the careers of their heroes, and some complete a variety of exercises to find the jobs most suited to their skills, qualities and interests.

There is no such thing as an ideal job that is good for everyone. Each of us has different skills, qualities and aspirations. The ideal job does not necessarily mean becoming President of a company or making a lot of money. While one person may dream of starting and building a large business, another may dream of becoming a good teacher. Ideal jobs are specific to individuals. What one dreams to become may be a useless pursuit in the mind of another person. The important thing in career planning is to remember to move in the direction of your dreams. The person who is following the direction of one's dreams will always be satisfied by the work environment while another person who is working just to pay bills cannot wait for the next weekend or the day off from work.

You should do whatever you can to step into your dream job. It will allow you to be yourself on the job. You will do well in a dream job because it will reflect your personality and values. You will feel fulfilled and achieve something dear to your heart. Because a dream job reflects your skills and talents, you are likely to achieve more. Your dream job will keep you excited and motivated. It will allow you to do what you enjoy doing. It will make you feel good because you are doing something you enjoy and make valuable contributions. You will wake up each morning looking forward to the work day ahead rather than waiting for it to be over. It will provide you with a sense of fulfillment. It will enable you to do the work you love. It will allow you to utilize your unique skills and talents. And, it will give you a sense of accomplishment.

What This Book Is About?

1. **Review how Covid-19 has impacted jobs and the workplace:** The workplace we return to will not be the same as the pre-pandemic workplace. Remote work has become widespread, and much of it is going to remain in place in the post-pandemic days. Even working from traditional offices is quite different now as we follow new health protocols. Many people got really burned out during Covid-19 and there are now a lot of job seekers who are just wanting a job change. Recruiting, interviewing, and other aspects of hiring have become virtual at many employers. Workers will have to adapt, and sometimes upgrade their skills, to match the new job requirements.

2. **Explain the job search process:** Most of the book is devoted to the job search process and how it has changed due to the Covid-19 pandemic. The book

provides a framework to identify the personal skills you enjoy using and how to find jobs that match those skills. It explains changes in the workplace due to the pandemic and how you should prepare and execute an effective job search strategy.

3. **Provide guidelines for using the Internet:** The Internet is becoming an essential and increasingly important resource for job seekers to find job openings, conduct research, get job search help, and apply for jobs. The book describes the resources available on the Internet for job search and career development. Each chapter provides descriptions of the Internet resources and websites to help job seekers. Also included is a separate chapter listing links to the best available websites for career information.

4. **Discuss how to develop a successful and happy career:** The book provides techniques and strategies for maximizing your professional success. While a job may be short term, a career is always long-term. A career consists of a variety of jobs, with each job usually leading to a position of higher responsibility. Career development affects everyone regardless of age or position. It is an ongoing process that continues throughout one's working life.

5. **Suggest ways to overcome the roadblocks:** The Appendix includes a description of what I learned from a stunning setback when I was just 14 years old. The lesson I learned from that adversity quickly turned me from a poor student to a good performer. What I learned at the age of 14 became a springboard for my life, and provided me the guiding principles I have used throughout my business career.

Each of us has unique strengths. The moment we identify these strengths and find a suitable career, we are well on our way to becoming successful and making great contributions. I have included some suggestions to find your strengths and unleash your potential. The book provides a description of the various job search tools and techniques. As a business manager, I have interviewed hundreds of candidates and observed what makes some candidates more successful than others. As an executive recruiter, I interacted with hiring managers from large and small companies in the financial services industry and learned how they select their employees.

There are primarily two reasons why people are not able to get the jobs they want. First, they often apply for jobs for which they are not qualified. The most important part of job search is to identify your special skills, and focus on jobs for which you are well qualified. The second reason why people remain unemployed is that they do not know how to go about finding a job. They rely too much on the traditional job hunting methods such as sending out resumes in response to job postings. They do not know enough about networking and targeted job search to go after unadvertised positions.

This book provides insights into the essential steps that lead to a successful job search. It will help you to identify your special skills and capabilities, and show you how to go about finding the job you want. It will bring to your attention the latest research, the most desirable job search methods, and the best available resources on the Internet to help you find a job that matches your career needs and expectations.

The book also covers my personal story in career development. It describes how I agonized over the direction of my career while I was still employed in a good job. I did extensive research, developed a plan, and took the needed action steps. That process led to a career change that enabled me to start an executive search firm. And, that turned out to be the best job of my life. My story appears in the chapter on career development that provides guidelines on how to develop a happy career that will result in job satisfaction and personal contentment.

The road to a happy career always starts with the job you love. When you get a job that matches your skills and job interests, you are well on your way to a successful career. Such a career will result in job satisfaction, promotions, and financial rewards. The starting point is the identification of your personal skills. This book will show you how to identify the skills you enjoy using the most and provide a pathway to get the job that matches your skills.

I know from personal experience that the candidates who get hired are not necessarily the ones who can do the best job. **The jobs often go to those candidates who know the most about the job search process.** This book will help you to gain that knowledge. It provides a framework to conduct job search in today's environment. It provides the tools and techniques needed in each step of the job search process.

Enjoy the book and have a very happy career ahead!

Narinder Mehta
P.O. Box 547
Dover, MA 02030-0547
E-mail: jobsbook1@aol.com
LinkedIn: www.linkedin.com/in/NarinderMehta

CHAPTER 1

YOUR CAREER AND COVID-19

I can't change the direction of the wind, but I can adjust my sails to always reach my destination.
—Jimmy Dean

The future of work is not going to look like anything we have seen before. The workplace of the pre-pandemic days is not the environment we are going to come back to. **The impact on jobs and the workplace has been the most significant among the economic costs of Covid-19.** Millions of people all over the world lost jobs and millions had to adjust to working from home. Yet millions of others who continued to work in essential places such as hospitals, pharmacies, and grocery stores had to follow new protocols to reduce the spread of coronavirus. Most of us have never experienced a global health crisis like this. We have never been forced to hide in our homes for long periods to avoid being infected or infecting others.

Since the pandemic started spreading around the world, working from home has become the catalyst for the way we work and live. The events of the pandemic have turned workplaces upside down. The boundaries between home and workplace have started to disappear. The pandemic has increased the challenges the workers already faced. This has also created many challenges for employers to cope with and manage a huge and totally unexpected change.

From remote work, we are going to shift to hybrid work, a mix of office and remote work. Some days you will go to the office, and other days you will work from home. Companies will have to bring some white-collar workers back into the office while allowing others to continue to work from home. Such arrangements will create complications. Employers will have to figure out new work schedules and configurations of office space. They will have to decide where people would sit in new offices and how they will interact. They will need to develop detailed plans, policies, and guidelines, and share that with employees to gain their confidence and support.

Employers will have to take whatever steps are needed so that people working from home still feel part of the team. While most employees have enjoyed working from home, many of them have missed the face-to-face interaction and companionship of working at the office. Training and onboarding would be more challenging in a hybrid environment. While it started out as a health crisis, this pandemic has created long lasting changes in our lives. It has affected the way we shop, the way we pay for what we buy, the way our children are getting education, and how we interact in the business environment as well as socially.

Right before the pandemic hit us in March 2020, the rate of unemployment in the United States was 3.5 percent. Just about anyone who wanted a job could get one. Covid-19 hit us with unbelievable viciousness and speed. Within the first 3 months of the pandemic, more than 40 million workers were unemployed. Millions more saw a reduction in work hours, benefits, and pay. The pandemic hit workers at all levels. But the most affected were the lower wage earners who were least able to absorb the shock of no paychecks.

Millions of jobs lost during the pandemic will never come back. On the other hand, millions of new jobs will emerge to meet consumer demand. These new jobs will require upgraded skills as automation and artificial intelligence will create additional requirements for skills needed. When you are ready to learn new skills to meet new challenges, enormous opportunities lie ahead.

Several industries are seeing increasing demand. These include healthcare, grocery stores, food companies, technology and development, logistics and transportation, online shopping, delivery services, financial services, cyber security companies, online learning companies, and remote meeting and communication companies such as Zoom. Amazon and Walmart have added thousands of jobs, and will probably add thousands more in the years ahead.

Covid-19 has substantially impacted three areas in our economy: digital commerce, telemedicine, and automation.

Digital commerce was already spreading and reducing sales at retail stores. The pandemic has accelerated that trend. Millions of people started shopping online out of necessity, and soon realized its ease and benefits. That trend is going to continue.

Telemedicine was starting to gain some traction, and got a big boost from Covid-19. This was sparked by fear of going to medical offices and emergency rooms, and some doctors were just not available for face-to-face consultation. Virtual interactions between doctors and patients are likely to continue.

Automation will continue to increase. We will see more and more products move from factories to consumers without much human contact. There is a sharp increase in the use of digital tools. The number of people using Zoom increased from about 10 million to more than 200 million within the first three months of the pandemic. One fortunate aspect of our current world is digital sophistication. We have networks that connect us virtually all over the world. We have networks of devices, software, and technologies that allow us to work remotely.

An area going through major change is how we pay for what we buy. People prefer to use plastic these days. My personal usage of credit cards has substantially increased since the pandemic. Now I rely more on online shopping and use credit cards to pay. Another trend is towards contactless payments where the users simply touch their cards to a terminal. This shift is likely to grow and become permanent. Companies in credit card business and financial services will continue to grow.

The pandemic caused businesses and consumers to adopt new behaviors. Some of these behaviors are likely to continue. Most of the people who started using digital channels for the first time during the pandemic are likely to continue using them when things get back to normal. Online transactions such as telemedicine and ordering groceries, food, and other essentials online are likely to continue. We achieved digital transformation in weeks which would normally take years to accomplish. The companies offered new ways of shopping from home and consumers responded quickly. We saw an explosion of home delivery services and curbside pickup of online orders.

Working from Home

The greatest impact of Covid-19 on the workplace is the sudden increase in employees working remotely. Remote work is here to stay perhaps at a lower level than at the peak of the pandemic. It has become a standard operating mode for most employers. Before the pandemic, it was hard to implement remote work widely as companies worried how it would affect productivity. When the pandemic hit, millions of workers were sent home to work remotely. Although working from home during the initial phase of the pandemic was a haphazard process, it has become better organized and more productive.

More people are working from home than the businesses ever planned for. Remote work is used more in some sectors such as technology, insurance, and finance. It has shown companies a way to lower costs and more effectively attract the needed talent. The shift toward working from home is a structural shift that would reshape the economy.

Remote work is also going to reduce business travel as the videoconferencing technology has demonstrated its value and virtual meetings have become widely accepted. This would have significant impact on airlines, hotels, and other segments of the hospitality industry.

Some work cannot be done remotely. This includes many jobs that require physical presence such as helping customers in a store, working with machinery, and providing certain services. It is estimated that more than 60 percent of employees in the US cannot work remotely. The share of work that cannot be done remotely is even higher in developing economies. Some of the work that can be handled remotely is done more effectively in person.

As we look to the future of work, many employers are planning a hybrid model that combines time in the office with remote work. For those considering working from home regularly, a dedicated space should be set aside to focus on work. This office space should be secluded from distractions such as TV and any noise from within the house or from outside. It will be nice to design a work-friendly space in your home that takes advantage of natural light and fresh air from windows and doors. Selection of your office chair and desk, and the needed equipment, should be done carefully.

Road to Recovery

We have recovered from some of the damage caused by the pandemic, but the next stages of recovery are going to be difficult. The pandemic is creating some fundamental shifts in the way we spend and how companies do business, and some of those shifts are likely to be permanent. It will take a long time to get back the jobs lost during the pandemic. After the 2007-09 US recession, it took more than six years to return to the jobs peak. The unemployment rate in the US rose to 14.7 percent in April 2020. This is the highest level since the Great Depression and is far greater than the 10 percent unemployment rate at the peak of the 2008 recession. While unemployment rate has reduced substantially, it is still far above the 3.5 percent unemployment rate just before the pandemic. The job market may not return to the pre-pandemic levels for some time.

We have an immense challenge ahead. The full recovery would not happen until we are able to control the coronavirus. The recovery would depend upon how safely the schools and businesses reopen and how people return to eating out, traveling, and attending recreational activities. There will be a sharp economic recovery when we are able to control the virus.

We will see growing use of artificial intelligence (AI) in business operations. Virtual agents can improve contact center efficiency and enable human agents to attend to more complex tasks. It is important to keep phone call wait times for customers within reasonable limits. When wait times are too long, customers tend to move to other suppliers. Many customer centers already employ virtual agents to handle unanticipated increase in workloads. AI's importance to companies is likely to increase in future years.

Searching for a Job

The rules of searching for a job have changed substantially during the pandemic. Virtual hiring process was in the early stages of development in the pre-pandemic days, but it has quickly become the norm. Rather than letting these changes overwhelm you, use them to your advantage. Now that more companies are working remotely, you may be able to apply for jobs that may have been out of your reach because of location. There are many new opportunities arising from new technologies sparked by Covid-19. Those who move ahead with care and thoughtful planning will certainly succeed.

The pandemic has certainly changed the workplace and what the candidates need to do to get the jobs they want. The old methods of job search have been replaced by new technologies. **Even before your resume is seen by a human, it needs to satisfy the software that screens candidates. The screening software is driven by keywords most relevant to a job.** Resumes that include such keywords end up on top of the pile. Once your resume is in the hands of a recruiter, it will get an initial scan for just a few seconds to determine if it deserves further consideration. It is a good idea to include a summary at the top of the resume that shows how you match what the job requires. Display what you have accomplished instead of using flowery language. Resumes that get attention are written in a format that is concise, easy to follow, and highlights the results one has achieved.

To succeed in job search, you must come across as the most suitable candidate for the position. Coming across as the second-best candidate won't do. How do you come across as the best candidate for the job? This book will show the steps you need to take to accomplish that.

Before we embark on job search, we need to define what kind of jobs would match our skills and job interests and give us job satisfaction. Then we need to find places where such jobs exist. We need to put together resumes and cover letters that will get us job interviews. When we get the job interviews, we must demonstrate how we match the job requirements. And, when a job offer comes, we need to evaluate it to determine whether it fits our near term as well as long term career goals. The level of our success will depend upon the effort we put into planning and preparation.

Determine what you want to do and develop a clear picture of why you want to do it. Once you know what jobs match your skills, you need to research your target industry and identify companies that match your requirements. You need to identify contacts in your target companies, and research your network to see who can introduce you to people in those companies to gain further information.

You can improve your job search effectiveness by developing a plan and diligently implementing it. Your plan should include specific action steps with completion dates. You will need a daily and weekly schedule of things to do that will move you in the direction of completing your job search. This plan must be written, and it should be reviewed and updated at a minimum of once a week. The job hunters who have a plan look upon job search as full time job, and dedicate about 40 hours a week to job search. Those without a plan approach job search haphazardly. They look for jobs in unorganized and inefficient ways, and therefore, they are not able to find the jobs they want.

I am going to give you a framework for achieving success in job search. It is based on many years of my experience as a business manager responsible for hiring employees. It is also based on my experience as an executive recruiter focused on finding management talent for client companies. The steps I am going to describe are inter-related, and one must take all steps to achieve successful results.

Here are the five essential steps in the job search process:

- **First and foremost, you need to identify your skills and job interests and then determine the career you want to pursue.** Self-knowledge is an essential step in job search as it helps to define the job you want. People who can find the right fit are happy and successful because they are doing what they enjoy. You have enormous potential, and you need to channel your energies in areas of your strengths. You need to put yourself in a career that will pull you in the direction of the greatest personal fit. No two individuals are identical; every person has a different set of skills and talents. It is extremely important to identify your specific strengths and how these match the available career options. Your performance will be superior when you are in an occupation you enjoy. Financial rewards and job satisfaction will follow when you are doing what you enjoy. Before beginning your job search, you need to define what you can offer to prospective employers and where you want to use your skills. Targeting your search to jobs that match your skills and background would certainly increase your success.

- **Second, you need a resume, online profiles, and cover letters that highlight your special skills and value to potential employers.** The purpose of online profiles and resumes is to get invited for job interviews. They demonstrate how you will be able to benefit your future employer. Every resume is unique depending on the qualifications and needs of a candidate. A well prepared and tailor-made cover letter is a tool to draw attention to the most relevant information in the resume. Think of it as a requirement when you send a resume. A cover letter confirms that you have read the job posting, understand the requirements, and you are well suited for the job. It is an opportunity for you to link your experience with the advertised job, and to provide any information specifically requested in the job posting that might not be included in your resume such as job location preferences.

- **Third, you need to identify and contact potential employers who may have job openings that match your skills and interests.** Once you have prepared a resume that shows your skills and abilities, the next step is to bring it to the attention of those who are responsible for hiring. Remember that posting your resume on one or more job-boards is not enough. You should identify several employer organizations and connect with them to find a suitable job. Targeting companies of special interest and networking are the two most effective methods of finding suitable jobs.

- **The fourth essential step is to get job interviews, prepare for interviews, and perform so well that you will be judged as the best candidate.** You should apply only for jobs for which you are well qualified and then tailor your resume and cover letter to the needs of potential employers. If you do this right, there is high probability you will be called for job interviews. A person is invited for the job interview only when the employer thinks there is a match with the job requirements. Your success in the interview process will depend on the level of your preparation. You should anticipate what questions are likely to be asked during the interview, and know how you are going to answer those questions. You should have a list of questions you want to ask the employer. The interview is an opportunity for you to learn about the job and the company so that you can decide whether it is the right opportunity for you.

- **The fifth essential step is to negotiate the job offer.** You need to evaluate the job offer to make sure you are getting a compensation package you deserve. When you are offered a job, you must make a decision that will have a long-range impact on your career path. This is an opportunity for you to define what you want and what you can get, and then negotiate an employment package acceptable to you. You can negotiate the job responsibilities, base salary, bonus, relocation package, benefits, severance terms and anything else included in the job offer. You need to research, consider alternatives, plan and effectively communicate with the employer. Remember that negotiating is a two-way process when both you and the employer try to reach an agreement that will be beneficial to both sides.

Preparation for Job Search

Your job search preparation must include the following two elements: Define the Job You Want and Your Key Message; and then develop a list of Potential Employers.

Define the Job You Want and Your Key Message

This is a statement of the kind of job you want based on a clear understanding of your skills and interests. It tells your prospective employers what you are looking for. You may define it by picking a job title such as "Sales Representative" or by selecting a range of job titles such as "Marketing Management". This would help you in putting together your resume and cover letters. By focusing on jobs that match your skills and interests, you improve the chances of finding a suitable position.

In addition, you need to develop the key message you are going to convey to prospective employers and to those in your network. This message describes how you are a good candidate for the position you are pursuing. You should put your key message in your resume and repeat it again and again in job interviews. That means going beyond determining a job title or cluster of jobs that will suit you. Prepare a key statement that describes you to prospective employers. Good key message makes employers want to talk to you. Many outplacement firms advise candidates to always develop a sales pitch and practice it often.

Prepare yourself to answer the question that often comes up in job interviews: "Why should we hire you?" This question is a test of your ability to select the relevant portions of your background to show how you meet the job requirements, and present that information clearly in a two-minute presentation. You should write such a statement, practice how you will deliver it in job interviews, and review it carefully to use in your resume.

To prepare your key message, you need to go to your list of accomplishments and skills and then describe your strengths to do the job you want. You need to focus on your desired job when preparing your key message. It should provide evidence that you can effectively handle the job you want. You should state your skills, personal qualities, experience and accomplishments that support the cluster of jobs that you are seeking. Your key message will guide your communications including resume preparation, conversations with contacts in your network, and job interviews.

Preparing a list of your skills and linking your skills with stories of accomplishments is a good way to begin to develop your key message. As you proceed with your job search and share your key message in your conversations and written communications, you will certainly find ways to refine your message and present stories of your accomplishments. Keep your target audience uppermost in your mind when you prepare and revise your key message. Discuss your key message with some friends, and particularly with two to three professionals in your field, who can give you an objective assessment.

Most people underestimate their value. They do not realize the skills and experience they bring to the table. You need to present your qualifications fully to get the kind of job and compensation you deserve.

Develop a list of Potential Employers

Once you have identified the job you want, you need to determine where you want to work. This exercise will lead you to the development of your target list of prospective employers. Your interest and preferences play a key role in developing such a list. You may prefer certain target employers because of where they are located, type of industry, the employer's size, and other factors.

Some people do not want to relocate and have strong preference as to where they want to live. That puts a limitation on where they can work. Another consideration is your choice of industry. While some occupations may limit your choice of industries, many other occupations allow you to work in a wide range of industries and locations. The size of a prospective employer (number of employees, annual revenue) may not be important in your search. On the other hand, some persons like to work for big companies with a lot of employees and resources while others prefer small organizations. If the size of a company is an important consideration for you, you will need to keep this in mind when picking your list of target companies. Some small companies and start-ups may offer huge compensation to attract outstanding talent. Check to make sure they have the resources to meet such commitments before you put them on your target list.

Having a target list of prospective employers will enable you to tap into the unadvertised job market. Keep in mind that more than fifty percent of jobs get filled without ever being advertised. When you have a target list of employers, it gives you the ability to talk to selected employer organizations. This will also enable you to make a better use of your network. You will have a list of your desired employers with you to share with contacts in your network.

When preparing your target list, focus on companies that are well suited to your skills and fields of greatest interest. This is a list of companies you want to work for; not a list of job openings. If you need help in developing your target list, go to the Internet and search the directories for information on industry, location, and size of companies you want to work for. My suggestion is to start with a target list of 25 prospective employers, and then gradually add or delete as you move forward with your search.

Once you have your target list, you need to research each organization. You can do so by going to their company websites and reading information available on the Internet. The publicly traded companies have annual reports that you can access on the Internet. You may also obtain additional information about any company by putting their name in one of the search engines such as Google. There are also specialized websites that provide profiles for companies in a variety of industries. The best way to get information about a target company is to talk to some of their employees. As you gather information about companies on your target list, you can use that information to rank your targets, and establish your priorities.

While the job market is tight, there are still millions of jobs for which companies are looking for suitable employees. New employees are being hired every day. Employers are always in need of experienced individuals who can step into a wide range of jobs.

Employment structure is changing

Just 50 years back, most of the work force in the United States was employed in factories. Now only a small portion of the labor force works in manufacturing. The employment structure will continue to change due to the impact of Covid-19, developments in technology, and in response to market needs. The long-term shift in employment from goods-producing to service-providing sectors is expected to continue.

Most jobs are not simply lost; instead they transform into new roles and opportunities that are shaped by new technologies. For example, telephone operators and receptionists were essential in every office, big or small, just a few years back. Now those jobs have almost disappeared, but new opportunities in data analysis and market analytics have emerged due to the need to process large amounts of business intelligence data. I remember how important it was at one time to have good administrative assistants to help in performing clerical tasks. Successful executive assistants in today's job market take on more challenging and intellectually stimulating roles by helping managers gather, analyze, and communicate the information necessary for planning and monitoring critical business operations.

You may want to visit the website www.onetonline.org for detailed descriptions of the world of work for use by job seekers. Another good source of information is www.glassdoor.com. It has millions of personalized jobs, salary information, company reviews, and interview questions posted anonymously by employees and job seekers.

Technology is changing rapidly

Advances in technology are taking place at a rapid pace to enable companies to work smarter with fewer resources. The prices for information technology and telecommunication services are coming down. More and more people have access to the Internet. The advances in technology have given us instant access to vast amounts of information at a low cost, and enabled companies to operate effectively with flatter and leaner organizations. We are becoming an information-rich society. We are entering an age where massive amount of data is coming from every direction. Good career opportunities are available for those who comprehend and manage the new technology. Continuous life-long learning is a requirement to succeed. Those who stop learning and growing will face road blocks.

Job changes will happen frequently

The average person will change jobs and careers far more frequently than persons in previous generations.

You should expect to change jobs several times in your work life, and that means you must continue to acquire new skills to meet the demands of new jobs. Companies will continue to make job cuts to manage costs and improve profits. On the other hand, an individual employee's sense of loyalty to the employer organization will continue to lower in the face of job cuts and increasing availability of new career options. Our workers now have higher levels of education than ever before. When we think of workplace today, we no longer think of it as a factory assembly line. Tomorrow's work will be focused less and less on repetitive processes, and more and more on collaboration and innovation.

In today's dynamic environment, we need to look for job security for workers, not for security of specific jobs. That means we should be training our workers to acquire new skills and knowledge to move from one job to another. This may mean learning computer usage, a new language, or some other skills to prepare for another job. The technical changes and the evolution of new businesses are always creating the need for new skills. Also, we need a change in our educational system to reduce excessive specialization. We need to teach people the skill of learning to learn so that they can move from obsolete jobs to the jobs in demand.

Continue to increase your value

You should continue to acquire new knowledge and skills to build and grow your career. Those who upgrade their skills and navigate their careers in the post-pandemic market place will have tremendous career opportunities.

Workers in the post-pandemic economy will require new skills and new knowledge to succeed. They will require on-going training and education to remain competitive in the changing environment. Each individual worker must be willing to take personal responsibility to increase one's value in the changing environment. You can make yourself the most sought after worker by acquiring the needed education and occupational skills.

Here are some strategies you can employ to build your career.

- **Adopt continuous learning and flexibility**. These are essential requirements for career development. We are surrounded by change. Many of yesterday's jobs have disappeared, and many jobs today did not exist a few years back. You should continue to acquire new knowledge by reading professional publications and participating in seminars and training courses.

- **Focus on your skills and areas of interest.** Identify what you are good at doing, and build those skills further. Tune up your skills to adapt to new environments. An open mind and the desire to collaborate with people will make your skills more valuable in the marketplace.

- **Develop the ability to market yourself.** This means knowing your skills and areas of competence, and effectively presenting what you can offer.

- **Create high quality online profiles, resume, and cover letters.** There is a full chapter in this book devoted to the preparation of online profiles, resumes, and cover letters.

The Internet has revolutionized communications around the world. The confluence of democratized knowledge, political reform, free trade, and economic development have torn down the walls that prevented small companies from participating in the world economy.

When I founded Mehta Consulting as an executive search firm in 1997, my intention was to limit operations to the United States. After I was in business for 5 years, one of my clients asked me to find a manager who would be willing to relocate from the United States to Jamaica to manage their call center operations. I successfully completed that search by finding a qualified candidate. A year later, the same client came back and asked me to find another manager for the expanding operations in Jamaica. Again, I searched and submitted a suitable candidate for that position. Then I received a phone call from a company that had recently established a call center in the Philippines. They asked me to find a manager who would be willing to live in the Philippines for a couple of years to manage their call center. I submitted an excellent candidate for them who moved from Boston to Makati City in the Philippines. That led to an on-going relationship to find additional candidates for that client's call center in the Philippines. **Because of the Internet, it has become easy to serve customers in countries far away from where one is located.** Although I was a small business owner, based in Massachusetts, my company established a global reach and served clients in several countries.

There is no question that American workers can thrive in the global economy. But it is going to require hard work and initiative. You should think globally to survive. This requires taking control of your career development, acquiring new skills, and maintaining a positive attitude to succeed in the new environment.

Success is a matter of Choice

Success in job search is a matter of choice; it does not happen by chance. Begin the job search process with a firm belief that you will get the job you want. When you are confident in your ability, it will be reflected in the way you approach employers.

Look upon job search as your entry into a competition. You are competing against all others who want the same job. Your success will depend upon proving that you are a better fit for the job than any other candidate. It is essential to highlight your skills and experiences that match the job requirements. Find ways to give yourself an edge as employers compare you to other candidates.

I would like to share with you the story of a 16-year old boy who decided to look for a job. He saw an ad that appeared interesting. The job vacancy ad asked candidates to show up for interviews on the following Monday. The 16-year old boy arrived at the place of interview, but was surprised to see about 20 candidates already lined up ahead of him. They were neatly dressed, and looked smart. The 16-year old boy thought to himself that if he was doing the hiring, he could hire any one of them. But he was not there to do the hiring. He was there to get himself hired. He started thinking about what he could do to change the odds in his favor. A bright idea came to him. He took out a piece of paper and a pen. He wrote a note, folded it neatly, and took it to the receptionist, and said: "Could you please give this note to your manager immediately". The receptionist opened the note, read it, smiled, folded it back, and took it to the manager who was doing the hiring. The manager opened it, and burst out laughing. Here is what the note said. It said: "I am the 21st boy in line. Please do not offer the job to anyone until you have seen me." Because of his initiative, he changed the odds in his favor. During the interview, he demonstrated how his qualifications fit the job requirements, and he did get the job. The moral of the story is that success in job search is a matter of choice. It is not a matter of chance or luck. You need to determine what you want to get, and then make the required effort to accomplish your goal.

Focus on your special skills and interests

You need to develop self-understanding to move your career in the direction of the right match, and to steer towards a job that fits your strengths and passions. Your personal values and goals should be at the heart of making career decisions that should fall within the framework of three considerations: job satisfaction, lifestyle suitability, and meeting compensation requirements.

The most successful people do not necessarily have the highest academic credentials nor do they make the highest amount of money. They are not always in the top management positions. **Successful people are those who are doing what they enjoy.**

Don't be afraid of failures because failures are the stepping stones to success. When you learn from failures, you will always emerge as a stronger and more accomplished individual.

We have the power to set the direction of our lives. It begins with finding a job well suited to our skills and job interests. We struggle to decide what to study in college, but we don't pay enough attention to deciding what is the right job that will make us happy and successful. We spend enormous amount of time and money on our education, but then end up accepting the first job that comes along. We accept whatever job is available, and then we are not satisfied. A great percentage of adult population has low job satisfaction.

The way to succeed is to steer your career towards opportunities that you are good at. It may sometimes require walking away from job offers that others would consider as great career opportunities. It is important to remember that all of us have unique strengths. We must set our own career goals that are consistent with our likes and aspirations.

A great career lies at the intersection of what you love to do and what are your greatest strengths. When you get what you love, make the most of it. Go the extra mile to achieve results that will enable you to move into positions of increasingly higher responsibility.

The number one thing that determines your success at workplace is the ability to connect with people. Only some of your success is determined by your education and technical skills. Most of your success comes from connecting with and influencing your boss, fellow employees, and your clients. You should come across as someone who is trustworthy and delivers what is promised.

One great lesson from Covid-19 is that we can adopt new ways of working and new technologies much faster than we ever thought possible. I am an optimist. I believe new opportunities arise with the dawn of a new day. We have had many major disasters, but we always manage to emerge stronger and more innovative. We have faced many challenges prior to Covid-19 including the pandemic of 1918, World War II, the Great Recession between 2007 and 2009, and have always emerged stronger. The coronavirus pandemic may also turn out to be a time in history that made us stronger, more resilient, and more prosperous people.

CHAPTER 2

MATCHING YOUR SKILLS TO JOBS

Always remember that you are unique, just like everyone else.

—*Margaret Mead*

Career choice must be based on what fits your **skills, values, and job interests.** Your skills play a critical role in determining your success in a job. When your skills are well matched to a job's requirements, you are likely to be productive, successful, and happy. You should take an inventory of your skills before you start your job search. This chapter is designed to show how to assess your skills and conduct job search based on your skills.

Even before the Covid-19 pandemic, emerging technologies in automation and artificial intelligence were creating skill gaps in the workforce. The pandemic has made this more urgent. Employees must adapt to the rapidly changing conditions. They need to upgrade skills and sometimes acquire new skills to meet job requirements.

The pandemic has accelerated the process of change in the workplace. The use of digital technology and artificial intelligence was fast increasing even before the Covid-19 crisis. The trend has accelerated. The contactless economy is growing and that will increase the use of digital technology. Many occupations will shrink or disappear, and other occupations will see growing demand.

In the old days, automation and robotics were involved primarily in large scale manufacturing. Now they are affecting tasks in many service roles. You need to ask yourself if your skills and capabilities are up to date to thrive in 2021 and the years ahead. You may need upskilling to make you more advanced and more capable of doing what you do now or you may need reskilling to prepare you to do something new.

Skill requirements are changing. People who have the skills in demand will get hired and advance more rapidly. If you don't have the needed technical skills, make sure to get the skills. There are a lot of low cost training programs available to upgrade your skills.

If you can find the right fit, you will advance rapidly in your career. Money and rewards will follow when you are in a job you enjoy.

All of us have enormous potential when we can channel our energies in the areas of our strengths. You need to find what is unique about you and then get a job that connects your skills and interests with the right opportunity.

Self-knowledge is essential; it helps to define the job you want. When you know exactly what you are looking for, you are more likely to find a job close to your ideal. You should think of what you want to become, the job you want, the industry in which you want to work, the kind of co-workers you want to have, and the place where you want to live. Success is measured by happiness in your professional and personal life, and not by accumulating the most money or by achieving a top position.

There are two types of skills: hard skills and soft skills. Hard skills are technical knowledge and abilities that let you handle job related duties. You can acquire these skills through classroom training, online courses, through books and training manuals, and on the job. Their focus is on specific processes such as the use of tools, equipment, and software.

By contrast, soft skills are the personal traits and behavior you use in different situations. Soft skills are transferable skills as you take them from one job to another. They are part of your personality. They show up as your behavior in different situations. Some of the most desirable soft skills are: communication skills; interpersonal skills; leadership skills; planning skills; and production skills. Other top skills needed by employers include continuous learning, agility in coping with change, and critical thinking.

Awareness of the top skills you possess is necessary for writing your resume and preparing for job interviews. How you display your skills on your resume will determine whether you are able to catch the attention and interest of recruiters. They spend just a few seconds to look at a resume and unless there is a spark that ignites their interest, the resume is not picked for further consideration.

Finding the right fit will result in an extraordinary career for you. Remember, you are unique. You possess a combination of skills and personal traits that are exclusively yours; just like your finger prints. Your career choice must be based on your assessment of personal skills. Some people make career decisions based on what they think are hot careers or what others recommend to them. As a result, they end up in jobs they do not like.

You need to prepare an inventory of your skills, personal traits, knowledge, experiences, and preferences. You need to find out what you enjoy doing and what motivates you. You must identify your strengths and develop a plan to make good use of your strengths. As you prepare the inventory of your achievements, including the compliments received for your work, you will find a pattern emerging to show you what type of activities you are good at. Is it communicating, organizing, problem-solving, building things, playing sports? This analysis will point to skills and talents in you that will be good assets in your job search and career planning.

Make a list of your dreams, the things you would like to have. What is the gap between where you are and where you want to be? Do not make your decisions based on the glamour associated with a position, but based on an assessment of your own skills and desires. Be completely honest with yourself. Once you have decided on your career direction, you need to acquire the competency to succeed in it. You need to identify the information, skills, and preparation you need to become the best in your field.

You should develop a clear vision of what you seek. The clearer your view of your destination, the more likely you are to get there. Just as you must know your destination before you start your journey to get anywhere, similarly, you need to know exactly what kind of job you want before you start the job search. There are so many career choices out there, and each with different kinds of rewards. You must determine what is right for you. If you are clear about what you seek, you will be closer to finding it.

Prepare a statement of what you hope to achieve, contribute, and become.

Here are some ways you can develop a vision of what you want:

- Think of what you want to become, the job you want, the industry in which you want to work, the kind of co-workers you want to have, the place where you want to live, and the kind of life style you want. Focus on your desires and dreams. Now, take a piece of paper and write down what you have been dreaming to become.

- Go to a list of careers and pick the one that matches your skills and desires. There are several career lists available on the Internet, and you can easily find them by going to www.google.com or another search engine. Do not be misguided by hot careers. Concentrate on a career that is a good match with your skills and talents.

- A third way to identify your dream job is to think of all the people you know or have seen or read about and whose job you would like to have. Now, pick two names from this group whose skills and strengths are close to your strengths. Take two sheets of paper, and write down in detail why you would like to have a job just like their jobs. Try to reach out to those people to learn more about their daily activities and how they have managed their careers. Many successful people enjoy the opportunity to counsel young professionals interested in their fields.

- A fourth way to identify jobs suitable to your skills and talents is to take career tests. Many of these tests are available on the Internet, and some are available at no charge. You should plan to use several self-assessment tests to improve your self-knowledge and awareness, but remember, none of these tools is going to tell you exactly what job you should go after. All that these tests can do is to point you in the direction of your career aptitudes, and help you to avoid making career mistakes. The websites available for self-assessment include www.careergames.com, www.self-directed-search.com, and www.careerkey.com. Another possible resource is Clifton Strengths assessment. It uncovers your unique rank order of 34 Clifton Strength themes. It is available at www.gallup.com.

An essential step in finding the right fit is to identify your strengths, likes, and your skills and interests. You can do that by defining the skills you have acquired through jobs, education, extra-curricular activities, hobbies, voluntary work and social activities. You can refine this profile by going through various aspects of the current and previous jobs that you liked and disliked, and how your performance was rated by your supervisors.

SKILLS AND TRAITS

There are three types of skills and traits that are important in selecting your career.

Personal Traits: These are part of your personality and habits. They include qualities such as integrity, enthusiasm, punctuality, attention to detail, determination, persistence, reliability, getting along with others, and working under pressure. These are the traits employers would consider while deciding whether to hire a candidate. You should identify three to five personal traits that make you an exceptional worker, and then you need to highlight those traits in your resume, cover letters, and in the interview process. If your job will involve working remotely, employers also care about your self-discipline and ability to work in this type of autonomous environment.

Transferable Skills: Transferable skills are those skills that you have acquired during various activities in your life including jobs, education, sports, hobbies and other activities. These are skills, that you can transfer and apply to your next job. All of us have been acquiring skills since childhood. Transferable skills are not necessarily the result of job experience or college degree. We acquire these skills while participating in extra-curricular activities, playing sports, and doing volunteer work. These activities provide us a range of skills that we can use when we get a job. These are portable skills that we take with us as we move from one job to another job.

Job-Related Skills: These are skills specific to an occupation such as being a lawyer, surgeon, or an accountant. These skills are essential for meeting job requirements, and are acquired through education, training, and work experience. The quality and extent of your job-related skills, as compared to other candidates, will weigh heavily in determining your suitability for a position. You need to emphasize and demonstrate your job-related accomplishments to establish yourself as a superior candidate. Job-related skills are essential for getting the job you want, and you need to continue to develop and expand your job-related skills.

What Skills Employers Want

The top skill that the employers look for in their employees is the ability to learn. This is the foundation skill, and all other skills are based on it. In addition, employers look for strong communication and leadership skills. Another important skill desired by employers is the ability to work well with others. This includes both being able to convey your ideas and effectively listening to other people's ideas.

Employers will have other skills that they look for in an ideal candidate for an open position including problem solving and creative thinking, team work, negotiating skills, goal setting, leadership, and organizational ability. Every job requires a specific set of skills to perform job requirements.

One of the skills that will be required almost universally in the future is the ability for collaboration. You will need to collaborate within the company, and with suppliers and customers. Some of them will be operating in foreign cultures. If you have the talent for working with people of different cultures and backgrounds, you have what is needed for success.

Collaboration skills will be required for jobs in operations, sales, systems, research and development, security, and other functional areas. Global supply chains will be producing many more products in the future. This process will have to work efficiently and will require large numbers of workers with the ability for collaboration. Also, there will be greater need for integration of various business operations. Many new products will come from synthesis; creating value by putting together dissimilar parts.

What Traits Employers Want

In addition to skills, employers seek certain traits and values in their employees. Here is a list of personal traits the employers look for.

Integrity: Employers look for honesty and integrity more than any other value in their employees. Integrity is an essential requirement for building business relationships and providing good leadership.

Positive Attitude: Positive attitude is an essential requirement for success in any endeavor. Persons with positive attitude are the ones who get hired and promoted. You need to communicate your passion for work in your resume and cover letters and show it during the interview sessions. Attitude springs from within, and therefore, you must focus on positive thoughts that will drive your interactions. Attitude shows up in subtle ways when you are writing to prospective employers and when you are interviewing for jobs.

Humility: This is a trait highly desired by employers. Lack of humility makes it hard to work with others, and will often disqualify a candidate. You must be willing to accept and welcome when someone else has a better idea. In an interview, you should talk about how you can contribute to the overall organizational success instead of just your own abilities.

Persistence: Employers look for workers who are dedicated, love what they are doing, and will persist in their efforts until they reach their goals. Persistence means a burning desire to accomplish what you want. It means determination to keep moving forward no matter what setbacks are faced on the way to accomplish your goals.

Reliability: Dependable employees are essential for a company's success. Employers look for workers who have demonstrated that they deliver on what is required of them.

Loyalty: Employers look for employees who will be loyal and dedicated to the company. It is the foundation stone for long lasting relationships.

Self-Confidence: This is a trait you need to cultivate to achieve success in your profession as well as all other activities. You must believe in yourself to generate positive reactions from prospective employers. Confidence builds with every successful experience. Reflect upon your outstanding accomplishments, and how they made you feel happy and successful. Such reflections will always translate into greater self-confidence.

Innovation: There will be increasingly higher focus on innovation for success in future jobs. Many companies have started to ask their employees to devote a portion of their time on a regular basis to being creative. Some companies require staff members to devote a part of their work day to brainstorming and thinking about new ideas and projects, unrelated to current responsibilities. Many successful companies believe "out of the box thinking" is necessary to win in today's hyper-competitive, global economy.

TRANSFERABLE SKILLS

Transferable skills are not necessarily the result of job experience or college degree. Each of us has been acquiring these skills since childhood. We acquire these skills while participating in extra-curricular activities, playing sports, and doing volunteer work in addition to acquiring such skills from job experience and education. These activities provide us a range of skills that we can use when we get a job.

Transferable skills are those skills that you have acquired during various activities in your life such as jobs, education, sports, and hobbies. These are portable skills that you can transfer and apply to your next job. They are determined by analyzing past experiences and accomplishments. Think of everything you have done and identify how it is transferable to what you want to do next. As you make a comprehensive list of your skills, you will probably find that you have more skills than you realized. Your transferable skills are your primary strength, and you should use them as such in your resume and cover letters.

You need to make an inventory of your transferable skills. These are skills that can be taken from one job to another. For instance, if you have management skills, they can be applied to a position in any industry. The same is true for many other skills such as communication skills and planning skills. You need to evaluate your transferable skills to see how these skills match the requirements for a specific position.

Transferable Skill Categories

There are 5 broad categories of transferable skills.
1. **Communication Skills:** These skills represent the skillful transfer of knowledge and ideas including

speaking, writing, listening, leading group discussions, negotiating, interviewing, and persuading.

2. **Interpersonal Skills:** These are skills for handling human relations including developing empathy, counseling, motivating, and giving support to others. Interpersonal skills are necessary for resolving conflict in work situations and relating to co-workers.

3. **Leadership Skills:** These skills enable a person to lead individuals and groups to accomplish tasks such as selling ideas and products, delegating, decision-making, coordinating tasks, and managing change. Companies also want people who have agility and can cope with many changes at work.

4. **Planning Skills:** These skills provide the ability to find information and conceptualize future needs including forecasting, identifying potential problems and possible solutions, setting goals, and evaluating results.

5. **Production Skills:** These skills enable effective production including organizing, implementing policies and work plans, goal accomplishment, and developing a team environment.

Most people have no idea of their transferable skills. When you ask students about their skills, many of them would say, they have been studying, and therefore had no time to acquire skills. The misunderstanding about skills comes from not knowing the meaning of the word "skills". We start acquiring skills in our childhood.

Skills are not necessarily acquired from job experience, but can also be acquired from hobbies, participation in sports, and other extra-curricular activities. Your transferable skills are the building blocks from which your career will be shaped. The more clearly you can identify your transferable skills, the more successful you will be in career planning and job search.

Here is a way to help you identify your transferable skills.

- First, go through the following Table of Skills and prepare a list of skills that you possess and enjoy using.
- Second, rank your favorite skills in the last column. The skill you enjoy the most should have the number one ranking and so on.
- Third, make a list of the top five favorite skills you love to use.
- Fourth, describe each of your top five skills in detail with examples of how you used those skills and the results you accomplished.

Table of Skills

List of Transferable Skills	Check the Skills You Enjoy Using	Rank Your Favorite Skills
COMMUNICATION		
Describing		
Editing		
Explaining		
Interviewing		
Listening		
Negotiating		
Persuading		
Presenting		
Reporting		
Writing		

List of Transferable Skills	Check the Skills You Enjoy Using	Rank Your Favorite Skills

INTERPERSONAL

List of Transferable Skills	Check the Skills You Enjoy Using	Rank Your Favorite Skills
Advising		
Caring		
Cooperating		
Empathizing		
Mediating		
Persuading		
Reasoning		
Reconciling		
Selling		
Trusting		

LEADERSHIP

List of Transferable Skills	Check the Skills You Enjoy Using	Rank Your Favorite Skills
Achieving		
Believing		
Competing		
Delegating		
Delivering		
Directing		
Mentoring		
Motivating		
Organizing		
Winning		

List of Transferable Skills	Check the Skills You Enjoy Using	Rank Your Favorite Skills

PLANNING

Analyzing		
Anticipating		
Budgeting		
Comparing		
Evaluating		
Forecasting		
Innovating		
Predicting		
Preparing		
Researching		

PRODUCTION

Achieving		
Building		
Coordinating		
Designing		
Implementing		
Managing		
Persisting		
Scheduling		
Supervising		

Go ahead and make a list of other transferable skills you possess, that are not included in the prepared list, but you think are important for your job search.

Now make a list of the top five favorite skills you love to use. The one you enjoy the most should have the highest ranking and so on.

MY TOP FIVE SKILLS

1. _____

2. _____

3. _____

4. _____

5. _____

Describe each of your top five skills in detail. Think of some examples of how you used each skill in the past and the results you accomplished. Go into as much detail as possible. This list of your top five skills is going to be the springboard for your career planning and job search. The more attention you give to preparing this list, higher is the probability of your career success.

Your success in finding the right fit will depend upon the identification of your transferable skills and your ability to highlight those skills in your resume, online profiles, cover letters, and during job interviews. As you begin to put together your list of transferable skills, you will find that you have more skills and value to offer than you thought possible.

The secret of finding the right fit is to understand the skills and traits the employer is seeking and how your background and qualifications match the employer requirements. If you can demonstrate that effectively in your resume and cover letters, job interviews will follow. That usually is the starting point for landing the right job.

The following two exercises will help you prepare for your job search.

First exercise, define **THE CAREER YOU WANT.** This is based on what you can offer to potential employers. You need to go to your inventory of favorite transferable skills. These are skills you acquired as a student, in sports, and while working in jobs. If you possess a lot of skills, and have skills of high complexity, you have more chances of getting positions of higher responsibility. Please review your inventory of transferable skills, job related skills, and personal traits. These are the building blocks for the occupation in which you will be successful. Now make a list of your favorite subjects. If you cannot think of a favorite subject, ask yourself this question. You are asked to deliver a speech on any subject of your choice, and you are given just 15 minutes to prepare for that speech. What subject would you pick? This may help you to identify the field where you want to use your favorite skills. Once you know the occupation you want, and the field in which you want this occupation, you are ready to pursue your career. Based on your inventory of favorite transferable skills and your favorite fields of knowledge, you should prepare a description of your favorite career. As an example, if your favorite skill is working with numbers, and your favorite field is banking, you should consider working in the accounting department of a bank. It is a good idea to research the career opportunity that interests you. Talk to some people who are currently in that field. In addition to determining the fields of your greatest interest, you need to think about the places where you would like to live, the environment in which you would like to work, the kind of surroundings you would enjoy in your work place and in your free time.

Second exercise; define THE ACTION STEPS TO FIND A JOB WELL SUITED TO YOUR SKILLS AND INTERESTS. This exercise would help you to prepare a detailed list of companies that seem to match your skills and job interests. You can now begin your research to find out which of these companies would enable you to build the kind of career you want. Fortunately, the Internet has become a great resource for conducting such research. An essential part of this exercise is to identify the decision makers in these companies by name, job title, address, and phone numbers. This information will be of great help to you as you begin to take the needed steps to get the job you want. While these exercises are time consuming, they will put you on the path to a very successful job search. They will drive you in the direction of a career you love, and that is an essential requirement for success.

Talk to some of the people who are in the career you want to pursue. Try to connect with people who are working at a company on your target list or at another company in the same industry. Try to gain a sense of culture within a company. Some companies empower their employees and there are others that are very regimented. The same job, say Financial Analyst, can be a very rewarding job at one company or a boring job at another company. Talking to employees at a company of your interest would give you powerful insights into the company's culture and work environment. This may also open doors for you, and result in introductions to companies of your interest. You can use these resources to get information interviews on Zoom or another platform.

Devote the time and effort needed to identify your strengths, special skills and traits and describe what type of jobs will match your personality and skills. You will be amazed at how quickly job interviews come your way when you pursue jobs that match your skills. When you know clearly what contributions you can make, you will find that the employers are eager to listen to you.

CHAPTER 3

USING THE INTERNET RESOURCES

We are all now connected by the Internet, like neurons in a giant brain.
—Stephen Hawking

The Internet is a worldwide network of interconnected computer systems which enables users to communicate and exchange data. It allows millions of individuals in countries around the world to connect with each other and accomplish quick and easy exchange of information. The Internet is a central tool in today's information age that enables us to use computers to transmit text, images, and sound. I remember the old days when I used to spend countless hours in reference rooms of libraries to find information I needed. That is no longer necessary. The information I need is readily available on my computer screen.

The Internet has become the gateway for instant access to information. It is a worldwide library which all of us can access at our convenience. All we need to do is to go to a search engine, type the subject of our interest in the search box, and a list of available resources will be displayed on our computer screens. There are easy links available on websites to read detailed information and find additional sources of information. Billions of people all over the world now use it and the usage is increasing at a rapid speed.

INTERNET AND JOB SEARCH

The Internet can help to find job openings, research companies, post resumes, learn how to conduct job search, and establish contacts with employers. It is a great resource for career information and for connecting with potential employers and recruiters.

In the pre-pandemic days, candidates looked for jobs online as well as by networking in person. Now even the networking needs to be done online. We have shifted to a complete reliance on the Internet. One needs to focus on job search through online resources such as major job sites, niche job boards, social media, and the employer websites. The Internet offers tremendous possibilities to find career opportunities and access tools to enhance job search effectiveness.

There are many websites available to help prepare resumes and cover letters, sharpen interviewing skills, and to get general help and advice for job search. Most of this information is available at no charge. Such help is available on job boards as well as many other websites including *www.job-hunt.org*, *www.jobhuntersbible.com*, *www.quintcareers.com*, and *www.rileyguide.com*.

The Internet is becoming an increasingly important resource for job seekers to quickly identify job openings. The available jobs are posted by employers and executive recruiters. The job postings appear on job boards as well as websites hosted by employers and executive search firms. There are plenty of job postings in just about every field and all geographical areas. These job postings are easy to find and you can locate them at any time of day or night.

JOB BOARDS

Job boards on the Internet contain job openings for candidates and resumes for employers and executive search firms.

Job boards have databases of job listings and resumes. They provide search functions to match the keywords in job listings with keywords in resumes.

Candidates get free access to job listings while employers and executive search firms need to pay a fee to list their jobs and to search resume databases. Employers select job sites based on how many and what type of candidates are visiting. They are looking for job boards that result in the most suitable candidates. It is the size of a job board and its specialization that determine whether an employer is willing to spend money to post jobs.

When employers want candidates from a special field, they sometimes go to job boards that specialize in those field. When I was doing executive recruiting, I would list my jobs with the big job boards such as career builder and monster, and with some of the specialized job boards. While I would get more resumes from the big job boards, often I was able to find the right candidates from the specialized job boards.

The big job boards or super sites have the largest number of job listings and attract the largest number of job seekers. In addition to the super sites, there are thousands of job sites on the Internet that list available jobs. These are specialized websites focused on specific occupation groups, industries, geographic areas and other segments of the employment market.

Here are some major websites for your consideration to post your resume.

www.monster.com

Monster is a global online service for people who need jobs and employers who need candidates. It started in 1994, and now provides online recruitment services in 50 countries. Monster acquired Hot jobs from Yahoo in 2010. Hot jobs was the third largest US job board. In addition to helping candidates browse for jobs, Monster offers many other services such as job-hunt strategy, resume preparation, and tips for interviewing.

www.careerbuilder.com

CareerBuilder offers a vast online and print network to help job seekers connect with employers. It is owned by a group of newspapers. It acquired Headhunter, a popular job board, in 2001 to create a recruitment resource for employers, recruiters, and job seekers. CareerBuilder is a leader in the industry in terms of visitors to its website. And, it offers useful tools and advice to job-hunters as well as recruitment resources to employers.

www.ziprecruiter.com

ZipRecruiter is an employment service founded in 2010. Employers and recruiters can post jobs to more than 50 job boards and social networking sites. They can also find and screen applicants in ZipRecruiter's resume database. ZipRecruiter enables job seekers to search active jobs on job boards and upload a resume and apply for jobs. ZipRecruiter alerts job seekers via email when a job matching a candidate's criteria has been posted.

www.craigslist.org

Craigslist has replaced the newspaper ads as the primary source for listing local jobs. It provides local classifieds for jobs. This is the place local employers turn to when they need to post a job. You need to go to the "jobs" section of craigslist to review job postings. Every large city in the United States has a craigslist site, and there are sites in many other countries. Every site has its own jobs section, and its own listing of jobs. You can just read the job listings in your area or search for jobs in various ways on craigslist.

Niche websites offer a good resource for job seekers who have identified their target industries and the positions they want to pursue. These sites provide job listings that target a specific type of job seeker. They help candidates to avoid having to sort through job listings that do not interest them.

Niche sites include www.careerrookie.com that offers resources to those who are starting their careers. They can search job listings, post resumes, and get job search advice. www.headhunter.com, a division of CareerBuilder, provides job listings and resources for those who are looking for jobs at management level. www.militarytimes.com offers job listings and employment related information for the military community. And, there are job boards for senior executives such as www.6figurejobs.com and www.execunet.com.

There are also industry specific websites. www.jobsinmotion.com is a job board specializing in the transportation industry. www.miracleworkers.com is a leading healthcare website listing jobs in the healthcare industry. www.moneyjobs.com is a niche website for banking, finance, and accounting jobs. www.sologig.com is a niche site for jobs in information technology and engineering. www.workinretail.com is a retail job board for information about job opportunities in the retail industry.

A comprehensive list of job boards as well as links to other career information websites are given at the end of this chapter. You will find these links very useful as you look for additional resources to help in your job search.

Keep in mind that there are several thousand job sites. In addition, there are thousands of company websites, recruiter websites, alumni groups and other websites listing job openings. Most of the websites are useful; some are not. Be very cautious whenever a website asks for a fee. You should be able to get most of the job search help and information at no charge.

Resume posting is a service offered by most job boards at no charge to applicants. Employers and recruiters need to pay a fee to access resume databases to search for suitable employees.

SEARCH ENGINES

You can find job postings in your field by going to major job boards as well as specialized job boards listed at the end of this chapter. In addition, you can locate job openings by going to job-related search engines that can help you in finding job listings of special interest to you.

Search engines use software tools called "crawler" and "spider" to comb the Internet to locate documents and their Web addresses, and indexing software to organize documents for easy access.

Considering that there are millions of websites, we need search engines to help us find the information we need. Google, Bing, and Yahoo are the three big search engines. In addition, there are search engines focused exclusively on jobs. These specialized search engines gather information from job boards, newspaper ads, and company career pages. And, they index such information so that it becomes available to you by job title and location. Some of the job search engines provide advanced information such as employment trends and salary information.

While a search engine would save you the time and effort of going to various job boards and career sites, keep in mind that search engines are free to determine which job sites they will search and index, and therefore, they may not be gathering information from job sites of special interest to you. While it is wise to use search engines to find information on job openings, you may still want to directly visit the job boards and other websites of your special interest.

www.indeed.com

This is a well-known search engine for jobs. It enables job hunters to find in one location jobs posted on job boards as well as company career sites. It gives them access to millions of jobs from thousands of companies. It is currently available in more than 50 countries. You can search for jobs, post resumes, and research companies on Indeed.

www.simplyhired.com

SimplyHired is a leading job search engine on the web. Their online database is built from searching thousands of job sites and companies. The website offers a salary calculator to help you compare your salary with others in your profession.

www.linkup.com

This is a job search engine that aggregates job openings found directly on company websites. It gives you access to un-advertised jobs on company websites. It is a free service for job seekers. When you click on a job opening, you are taken directly to the employer's website to get details about the job.

TAKE ONLINE TESTS

There are many tests available online to help you evaluate your personal traits and skills, and to offer advice on suitable occupations.

Most of the tests are self-directed, and some require assistance from a trained professional. Some of the tests are available free on the Internet, and others charge a fee. Online tests fall into two broad categories: personality tests and career tests.

Personality Tests

You may want to check the following websites for taking personality tests. Some tests cost money. There are many other online personality tests available at no charge.

www.myersbriggs.org

The Myers-Briggs Type Indicator (MBTI) is one of the most popular personality tests. It is an instrument to help you with a basic understanding of your personality type. The website explains where and how to take the MBTI personality assessment and get your personal one-on-one feedback.

www.keirsey.com

This website offers several self-directed tests. The Keirsey Temperament Sorter is their most widely used personality instrument. It helps individuals discover their personality type. It could help you develop a better understanding of yourself and how to find your career fit or get more satisfaction in your current job.

www.9types.com

This website explains the nine types of personality: Reformer; Helper; Motivator; Romantic; Thinker; Skeptic; Enthusiast; Leader; and Peacemaker. There is a sample test at no charge with 38 questions you can complete in 5-10 minutes to indicate your basic type.

Career Tests

While online tests can be helpful in giving you suggestions for careers to pursue, they rarely define exactly the career you should follow.

No test can tell you what career you should select. All that a test can do is to help you learn about yourself and identify some suitable careers to pursue. Never depend upon the results of a single test; plan on taking several tests to find the career direction you should follow. A variety of tests would give you a more balanced view of yourself and what type of career options you should pursue.

www.careergames.com

This is a colorful website with a lot of useful information presented by Daniel Porot, a leading European pioneer in career design and job-hunting. The information available on this website includes: self-assessment, job targeting, and interviewing. The self-assessment portion of the website is designed to help you uncover your hidden talents, explore the environment in which you thrive, and to help you find out what kind of people you like or do not like to work with.

www.self-directed-search.com

The SDS is a popular test developed by Dr. John Holland. His theory states that most people can be loosely categorized into six types – Realistic, Investigative, Artistic, Social, Enterprising, and Conventional, and that occupations can also be classified by these categories. The test takes 20-30 minutes to complete and costs $9.95. Taking the test could help you identify the careers that match your interests and abilities. But keep in mind that no one test can determine the career you should pursue.

www.careerkey.org

This is a good resource on the Internet created by Dr. Lawrence K. Jones, internationally recognized counseling psychologist. The career test is designed to help you match your personality with careers.

Conduct Research

Anyone with a computer and an Internet connection can access the worldwide library of information at anytime from anywhere in the world. This is perhaps the greatest contribution of the Internet.

To get the information, you need to know how to access it. Special websites have emerged to help us get the information we need.

www.refdesk.com

This is a good place to start your research. It provides you access to just about every resource on the Internet. It provides ready access to launch the three major search engines – Google, Bing, and Yahoo. It includes reference sites, directory access, dictionary and thesaurus, and latest news as well as stock quotes.

www.bizjournals.com

This is the online media division of American City Business Journals. It operates the websites for each of the company's 40 print business journals. Its archives contain 1.25 million business news articles, and it was characterized among the "Best of the Web" by Forbes magazine.

www.corporateinformation.com

This is a good place to get information about potential employers. While the basic information (such as company profile, business description, number of employees, stock performance, sales and revenue) is available at no charge, you have the option to purchase a full report.

www.forbes.com

Forbes magazine offers an online list of the Global 2000 companies listing their rank, country, industry, sales, profits, assets, and market value. You have the option to sort this list by industry, country, and other criteria. Forbes has several other lists on its website that could be helpful to you in researching potential employers.

Job seekers can conduct online research on jobs, companies, occupations, salaries, and cost of living differences for various cities. You can find names, titles, and contact information about persons you want to approach. Sometimes, you can even find detailed information about the persons you will be meeting for job interviews. Every job search requires some research, and the need for research increases as you look for higher level positions. The Internet was conceived to enable research. It is an easily accessible library with information on every subject. A good place to start your research is www.refdesk.com. It provides you access to just about every resource on the Internet. This resource includes reference sites, directory access, dictionary and thesaurus, and latest news as well as stock quotes.

Meaningful job search is about finding opportunities for which you are well qualified. Further, it is about researching the job and the hiring company, and submitting a strong resume and targeted cover letters that effectively show how you are qualified for the job. And, it is about preparing for job interviews and effectively handling interactions during face-to-face interviews. It is about negotiating a good salary and employment package that will provide you with rewarding and fulfilling work for many years.

The Internet is a wonderful research tool and source of information. You can use it to find suitable job postings and identify companies particularly suited to your job interests. You can research potential employers. The Internet does not take holidays and it does not go to sleep at night. It is available to you all the time at your convenience. You can quickly find the job postings for functional areas and geographic locations of interest to you.

Apply for Jobs

A vast number of job openings in all occupations and in every major city are available on the Internet.

While big job boards are good places to start your search on the Internet, always try to find some specialty job boards that cover your field of specialization and target market. Such specialty job sites may belong to associations and trade publications in your industry, and the executive recruiters specializing in your industry.

You can submit your resume online for most job postings. This is a great convenience, and at the same time, it can turn into a trap. Since it is easy to send resumes online, many candidates make the mistake of distributing their resumes indiscriminately. They apply for jobs for which they are not qualified. As a result, they do not get job interviews after sending hundreds of resumes.

The most effective way to apply online is to apply only for jobs for which you are well qualified and then submit targeted cover letters showing how your qualifications match the job requirements. You should paste your resume in the body of your e-mail and send it also as an e-mail attachment. Your resume should include the keywords employer is likely to use when searching the database. You may want to develop the list of keywords by reviewing the job posting and talking to some of your associates. You need to put together a list of keywords the employer is likely to use.

Post Your Resume

The Internet has websites that allow you to post your resume for review by employers and recruiters who want to fill open positions.

You can post your resume on job boards such as www.careerbuilder.com, and www.monster.com, as well as many other websites. Once you post your resume, it will go into a database that may be searched by employers and recruiters. It may also get posted on other databases. Therefore, make sure this is something you want to do, before you proceed. When you want to maintain confidentiality, use resume posting websites that allow you to withhold your name, street address, and phone number.

SOCIAL MEDIA AND THE JOB SEARCH

Social media is a new class of Internet sites, services, and applications that facilitate conversations between their users. The most popular and famous social network is Facebook, but there are hundreds of other social media websites that attract users based on their social affinity. Social media has transformed in many ways how people interact.

Using Social Media in Your Job Search

Social media can be an invaluable asset in all steps of the job search process including networking, finding prospective employers, creating a strong resume, preparing for interviews, and cultivating strong references.

Social media can be your most valuable resource for networking.

In the pre-pandemic days, the best way to meet and make an impression on new people was through face-to-face forums such as networking receptions and conferences. Today, with the help of blogs, Twitter, Facebook, LinkedIn, and other social media sites, it is possible to establish personal and professional relationships without ever meeting face-to-face. As a first step, consider starting a blog or a micro-blog. A well regarded and informative blog can be your most valuable networking asset. It is an ideal demonstration of your knowledge of a subject and your ability to communicate in writing, and it will be a catalyst to help you start conversations with your peers and leaders in your industry. A good blog has a purpose; do not create a blog that is an unstructured journal of your thoughts. Instead, pick a topic for your blog that you are knowledgeable about and that others will find valuable. For your blog to be useful and gain popularity, you should plan to post at least once a week.

Use your online network to find prospective employers.

It is true that the best jobs are taken before most people even know about them. This is because employers turn to their own network first when trying to fill a key job, and they feel much more confident hiring someone they know or someone that comes recommended from a trusted source. Start your job search by reaching out to your friends on Facebook and connections on LinkedIn. These resources will help you find positions that may not be listed yet. You can discuss with them the type of career you are looking for. You can tell them about the companies you have identified that interest you, and how you are proceeding with your job search. Ask them about any additional companies you might look at or how you might proceed with your job search.

Your online presence is a critical component of your resume.

Just as you must research companies online before submitting your application, hiring managers will often research a candidate online before extending an invitation for job interview. As a result, your online presence is a critical aspect of your candidacy and you must manage it with the same attention as your resume. Any information available online can and often will be used by recruiters in evaluating candidates. As part of the process of creating your resume, you should create a profile on LinkedIn that describes your experience accurately, effectively, and in sufficient detail. If you have a website or a blog, make sure your biographical information is up to date. If appropriate you may want to dedicate part of your site to your job search by including an online version of your resume or a portfolio of past projects and accomplishments. Be aware that employers may use any aspect of your online presence to evaluate your candidacy. Make sure that all aspects of your website and social networking profiles portray you in the best light.

Use your social network to prepare for interviews.

Before interviewing at a company, look on social media sites such as LinkedIn and Facebook to see if you know anyone that currently or previously worked at the company. You should consider reaching out to direct connections, and to friends of friends. Most people are willing to discuss their experiences when you are respectful of their time and do not pry into subjects that may be governed by confidentiality. Before each of these conversations, prepare a short list of questions to make sure that you can get maximum benefit from the opportunity. In some cases, making a good impression on a current employee can have a positive impact on your candidacy.

Use LinkedIn to cultivate your references.

LinkedIn has an invaluable feature that allows people to post recommendations for you to your LinkedIn profile. Prospective employers may use these recommendations to gain insights into what your peers think of you and how they describe your positive traits. While these recommendations will not take the place of personal references, they do provide an important source of information for hiring managers. LinkedIn recommendations can be a great way for you to start the process of cultivating a strong set of references. Follow these steps to cultivate your references via LinkedIn.

1. Begin by setting up your LinkedIn profile.
2. Establish your LinkedIn network by reaching out to those you know.
3. Select LinkedIn connections who you feel would be willing to create a recommendation for your profile.
4. Reach out to the list of LinkedIn connections with something like this: "I am in the process of seeking job opportunities. You are a trusted colleague and I would value your recommendation on LinkedIn." You may want to include some information to remind that person of projects that you worked on together and project accomplishments that you are particularly proud of.
5. Most often, only a subset of persons you approached will create recommendations for you. You will have the opportunity to accept or reject those recommendations.
6. Reach out to the people who took the time to create the best recommendations for you and ask them if they would be willing to act as a personal reference.

Making the Most of Social Media

Social media sites can be your biggest asset in finding and attaining your dream job. They provide an unprecedented way to strengthen your personal network and demonstrate the knowledge and skills that prospective employers are looking for. Creating a strong online presence takes time and dedication, but it is well worth the effort. Prospective employers and recruiters are increasingly relying on social media to find and research candidates. In the best case, you will find that the tables are turned – job opportunities will find you.

A Word of Caution

As with any powerful tool, using social media requires some caution. It is said that the Internet is written in ink, not pencil. Anything you do online is recorded, and you may not have the ability to control the dissemination of that information. Take care to post only that information which you would not mind sharing with current and future employers. It can be impossible to retract an ill-advised comment or inappropriate photo. If you wouldn't do it at work, don't do it online.

WEBSITES FOR CAREER INFORMATION

The Internet has made it easier for us to research topics related to job search and career development. There are many websites available to find career information. Most of them provide information at no charge.

Following is a list of some of the employment related websites.

Job Boards, Big Sites

www.careerbuilder.com

www.craigslist.org
www.monster.com
www.ziprecruiter.com

Job Boards, College Graduates

www.collegegrad.com
www.collegerecruiter.com
www.aftercollege.com

Job Boards, Freelancers

www.fiverr.com
www.flexjobs.com
www.freelancer.com
www.simplyhired.com
www.upwork.com

Job Boards, General Listings

www.careerbuilder.com
www.careerxchange.com
www.careerjournal.com
www.careerlab.com
www.careerrookie.com
 www.craigslist.org
www.dice.com
www.flipdog.com
www.monster.com
www.naukri.com
www.vault.com
www.ziprecruiter.com

Job Boards, Government Jobs

www.careersingovernment.com
www.federaljobs.net
www.governmentjobs.com
www.usajobs.gov

Job Boards, International

www.eurojobs.com
www.jobpilot.com
www.naukri.com
www.overseasjobs.com
www.planetrecruit.com
www.topjobs.net
www.monster.com

Job Boards, Niche Listings

www.allretailjobs.com
www.callcenterjobs.com
www.careerrookie.com
www.jobsinmotion.com
www.militarytimes.com
www.miracleworkers.com
www.moneyjobs.com
www.nicheboards.com
www.sologig.com
www.telecomcareers.net
www.workinretail.com

Job Boards, Senior Executives

www.6figurejobs.com
www.careerjournal.com

www.execunet.com
www.headhunter.com
www.netshare.com
www.theladders.com

Job Boards, Women

www.womensjoblist.com
www.careerwomen.com

Job Fairs

www.jobexpo.com
www.cfg-inc.com

Job Search Resources

www.glassdoor.com
www.job-hunt.org
www.jobhuntersbible.com
www.onetonline.org
www.quintcareers.com
www.rileyguide.com

Learning Resources

www.corporateclassinc.com
www.coursera.org
www.edx.org
www.linkedin.com
www.udemy.com

Networking

www.facebook.com
www.linkedin.com

www.people.yahoo.com

Online Testing

www.careergames.com
www.careerkey.org
www.careerstorm.com
www.imapmycareer.com
www.gallup.com
www.keirsey.com
www.myersbriggs.org
www.self-directed-search.com
www.vocrehab.com

Recruiter Directories

www.aesc.org
www.kennedyinfo.com
www.onlinerecruitersdirectory.com
www.searchfirm.com

Research Websites

www.bizjournals.com
www.corporateinformation.com
www.forbes.com
www.hoovers.com
www.refdesk.com
www.thomasregister.com

Resume Preparation

www.vault.com
www.monster.com
www.susanireland.com

www.resume-help.org
www.cover-letters.com

Resume Posting Services

www.executiveagent.com
www.forwardyourresume.com
www.resumedispatcher.com
www.resumerabbit.com
www.resumeviper.com
www.resumezapper.com

Salary Information

www.jobstar.org
www.salary.com
www.salaryexpert.com

Search Engines, General Purpose

www.bing.com
www.google.com
www.yahoo.com

Search Engines, Jobs Focused

www.indeed.com
www.jobster.com
www.linkup.com
www.simplyhired.com

Video Resumes

www.flexjobs.com
www.indeed.com
www.thebalancecareers.com

www.wyzowl.com

Visual Resumes

www.indeed.com
www.monster.com
www.pinterest.com
www.topresume.com
www.visualcv.com
www.zety.com

Using job search websites is one of the best ways to find career opportunities. There are hundreds of such websites, and they list millions of jobs organized by the type of job, industry, and location. They also offer a variety of tips and resources to help job seekers. You should plan to register with several websites as each offers some unique features. Also keep in mind that job websites are just one way to look for jobs. You should always pursue networking and other methods of job search.

We are very fortunate to have the Internet. This is a wonderful resource available to all of us and at no cost. You can use the Internet to prepare your resume, locate suitable job opportunities, research careers and possible employers, get job search help, and apply for jobs. Those who have learned to use this resource effectively are way ahead of others.

CHAPTER 4

ONLINE PROFILES AND RESUMES

The challenge of life, I have found, is to build a resume that doesn't simply tell a story about what you want to be, but it's a story about who you want to be.

—Oprah Winfrey

The Covid-19 pandemic has caused most employers to change their recruitment strategies. Employers are switching to virtual interviews and online talent assessment. Some companies are now handling their entire talent acquisition process remotely. Candidates submit their resumes online, and some are required to complete detailed questionnaires. Interviews are conducted over Google Hangouts, Zoom, Microsoft Teams and other platforms to get an assessment of the candidate's suitability for the job. This assessment includes the candidate's background and experience as well as the ability to communicate and interact. Some companies even train the new employees in a virtual learning environment through self-directed learning and group discussions in a video classroom.

The purpose of online profiles and resumes is to get job interviews. You state what you have achieved and how you can benefit the employer.

Before the Internet, a resume and cover letter were the only items available to an employer to determine whether a candidate should be called for an interview. Now that has changed. Employers are now able to find detailed information about a candidate by going to a search engine such as Google. All that a Recruiter needs to do is to type a candidate's name in the search box, and they are able to see what is posted on LinkedIn, Facebook, and other websites. They can see any comments and photos you have posted or that are posted about you. Most employers now check the Internet and evaluate candidates based on the information they find on Google and other search engines.

You should enhance your online presence by adding information that helps your credentials. Google your name and read information that appears about you on the Internet. Some websites such as LinkedIn allow you to complete a profile. Post your complete profile. Answer all questions and update your information as needed. Join professional groups on LinkedIn and other social media sites. Write a blog to show your expertise in a subject or post comments on blogs in your field.

Your resume is a statement of what you have achieved in the past and your capability for future accomplishments. It should highlight why the employer should want you, and include a description of your accomplishments, work experience, education, skills, and interests. It should be a summary of your top skills and major accomplishments and how you can benefit the employer.

Social network profiles have not replaced the resume. While your presence on social networks has become an important element in the job search process, it does not replace the need for an effective resume. In fact, a good resume is a starting point for putting together your profiles on social media. You should prepare your resume and online profiles in a way that you want the recruiters to see you. Recruiters will be looking for things that make you stand out from other candidates.

There are several social networking sites that maintain information about you. They include LinkedIn, Facebook. Twitter, and Instagram. In addition, when you have your own website, post a blog, or appear on the Internet in any other way, your information will become available to others. This information can help you, get you invited for a job interview, or hurt you depending on what appears about you on the employer's screen. Almost all employers will check information about you on the Internet before inviting you for an interview. Vast number of candidates have been rejected from consideration based on what appeared on the Internet. You can greatly increase your chances of getting a job by having good information on the Internet.

Posting Your Online Profile

You can post your online profile directly with the job boards. They pool and organize their resume databases so that employers and headhunters can search for suitable candidates. You should plan to create a text-only version of your resume that can be easily uploaded. If your resume has images or special formatting, it may not upload properly.

Almost every job board maintains a resume database. In addition, there are resume distribution services which post your resume on multiple databases. The resume distribution service providers include Resume Viper, Resume Dispatcher, Resume Zapper, and Resume Rabbit. Most of them charge a fee for their services.

Here are some of the best websites for posting your online profile. Detailed information about these websites and other resources is included in Chapter 3 "Using the Internet Resources".

LinkedIn: LinkedIn has evolved into the best platform for job search and professional networking. There is no charge for posting your profile on LinkedIn. LinkedIn also offers a premier membership with access to additional benefits including a list of those who viewed your profile, and the ability to send messages to people you are not connected with. LinkedIn encourages you to complete a detailed profile and gives you step by step directions to complete it and update it regularly. You should also consider posting a good professional photo.

Indeed: This is a great website for posting your resume. It is a free website. You need to set up an account to post your resume. Once you set up your profile to "public" the recruiters will be able to see your resume. When an employer is interested in speaking to you, they will send a message though Indeed. This website covers jobs in all industries and experience levels.

Monster: Monster provides recruitment services in many countries. You can look for jobs on Monster by job category and by location. In addition to helping candidates find jobs, Monster offers many services such as tips for resume preparation and for interviewing. Job search resources at their website include resume/cover letter templates, thank you note templates, and interview practice questions.

CareerBuilder: Career Builder offers a vast network to help job seekers connect with potential employers. It provides salary tools to help you compare your salary with others with the same job title in your area. You can also sign up for job alert emails to keep track of positions you are interested in.

Zip Recruiter: Zip Recruiter was founded in 2010. It is a marketplace for job seekers and employers. It enables job seekers to search for jobs on more than 50 job boards and social networking websites. It uses the data base to find the best companies for candidates and then sends them emails when a possible match becomes available.

College Grad: This is a good place to post your profile for entry level jobs. It is free to set up an account and post your resume. You can apply for entry level jobs across a wide range of industries.

Craigslist: This is a good place to look for local jobs. There is no charge for posting your resume, but the service providers pay a fee. It is available in many cities in the US and in several countries.

Dice: This is a leading database for tech jobs. It is used by major corporations to look for talent in IT, engineering, and computer sciences. It is a free website for candidates. It is a good place to post your resume if you are seeking a position in the tech industry.

The Ladders: This is a good place to look for high paying jobs. Its focus is on jobs that pay at least $100,000 per year. This website is widely used by recruiters to search for talent for their client companies.

Upwork: This is a website to get freelance work. About 5 million companies and millions of freelancers use this website. Freelancers in a variety of industries can find clients on this website. There is no charge for posting your profile, rates, and work samples. But you need to pay a percentage of your earnings when you get a client.

Facebook: This is the largest social media channel in the world. It is a place the recruiters use to evaluate candidates. Make sure that your profile and work history appear in a manner that you want to share with recruiters. Also include keywords in your profile that would bring it up when recruiters are searching for candidates in your area of interest.

Twitter: This is a place to show your knowledge in your field. You can send Tweets about news and events in your industry. You can retweet advice from experts in your industry. The way you present yourself can attract the interest of recruiters. You should make your Twitter profile professional and build your network of contacts. Also display a good professional photo.

Posting your resume online is a great way to connect with recruiters and employers. Most job sites are free for job seekers, but some have membership fees to access premium services. While each job site has its own unique features, most rely on keywords that recruiters will use to search for candidates for a designated position.

You should not rely exclusively on posting your resume. Plan to use at least three to four different methods of job search, and posting your resume should be just one component in that strategy.

Resume Objectives

While online profiles on social networking websites are becoming increasingly important, a good resume is still a vital part of job search. It is a statement of what you have achieved in the past and your capability for future accomplishments. It gives you a place to organize and summarize your personal information.

Resume has multiple uses: it helps you get job interviews, you can send it to people who are willing to serve as your references, you can have it readily available as a synopsis of your qualifications when you are doing phone interviews, and it is something you can leave with people you meet during your job search. This is the document you also use for posting your profile on major job posting websites.

In Chapter 2 "Matching Your Skills to Jobs" we discussed how to identify your skills and job interests to come up with your target jobs. Your resume should be prepared to focus on target jobs and highlight your top skills. This will help you to prepare a strong resume that will attract the attention of recruiters. Such a resume will use the keywords included in job postings for your target jobs and present your qualifications to show how you match job requirements.

The first step in this process is to select a title for the job you are seeking. Recruiters search resume databases by putting a job title and relevant keywords in the search box. Your goal is for your resume to come up when a recruiter is searching for candidates for your target job. How do you accomplish that? You want to make sure that the key words from the job posting are included in your resume and cover letter. You should review at least ten job postings in the category of your target job. You can get those job postings by going to any of the employment websites such as www.career.com, www.monster.com, and www.indeed.com. You should do a search for your target job to find out what qualifications employers are seeking, and what keywords they are using to describe their requirements.

It is true that social media profiles have become important resources for job search. But you still need an effective resume to succeed in the job search process. It enables you to organize your information and present it to prospective employers. LinkedIn, Facebook and other resources on the Internet have become essential in the job search process, but you still need a resume. Your resume will help you organize your information and effectively present it on social media websites.

A resume is a marketing tool for a candidate seeking a new position. Your resume and cover letter will be competing with hundreds of other applicants for a recruiter's attention to schedule interviews. To get that interview, it must be an exceptional document both in terms of content and presentation.

The purpose of a resume is to get job interviews. It is a statement of your skills and abilities to do the job for which you are applying. It tells the employer the benefits you offer, and how you will be successful in the position. The resume should have a good appearance so that the recruiters will pick it up and read it. That means it should be formatted properly, should have ample margins, and a formal type face. Remember, the purpose of a resume is to stimulate the recruiter's interest so that you get called for an interview. Your resume should appear professional and have relevant and valuable content. It should be short, simple, and easy to read.

Keep the objective of getting invited for job interviews uppermost in your mind as you write your resume.

It is a marketing document which demonstrates what you have accomplished in the past, and how that will help your prospective employers. Write your resume with great enthusiasm to create a document that you can be proud of. Everything you state on your resume must be true. Your resume is the bridge to reach your dream job. Although, most of the content of a resume is based on your current and previous jobs, it is not just a history of the jobs you have held. Your resume is an advertisement of your experience and accomplishments which has the sole purpose of getting you invited for job interviews.

Carefully checking your resume is a good first step. Also ask one or two persons to proofread your resume before sending it to prospective employers. Your resume should be free of any typing, spelling or grammatical errors.

Every job posting results in hundreds of resumes. Recruiters usually glance over a resume in a few seconds. The top half of the first page of a resume often determines whether a candidate gets any further consideration.

Remember, what you have done in the past is a good guide as to what you will do in the future. It is important to show in your resume how you created value for your past employers or how you saved money for them by improving products or services. Your resume should be a proposal of what you can do in the future, rather than just a statement of what you have done in the past. Every resume is unique. It is a marketing communication designed to win an interview.

Your experience level and the type of job you are seeking determine the type of resume you need. Someone who is just entering the workforce should focus more on educational background, as compared to another candidate with substantial work experience who should focus on job accomplishments. Review some of the sample resumes available on the Internet before putting together your own resume. Sample resumes are available on many job posting websites.

The most effective way to get interviews is to use an accomplishment based resume and then target it to specific job postings. Recruiters want to know what you accomplished in your previous positions, not just where you were employed. You need to demonstrate how you created value and saved money for your previous employers. You should provide instances of how you accomplished results, and try to attach a monetary value to what you accomplished.

Resume Types

There are three types of resumes: chronological; functional; and a combination of these two types.

Chronological Resume: This is the most common type of resume. It lists work experience and educational history in a reverse chronological order. The most recent information is placed first. The focus of this type of resume is on work experience listed in a chronological order starting with the current position. It begins with a statement of career summary and goes on to describe work history and accomplishments in each job. Recruiters prefer this type of resume because it demonstrates career progression of a candidate. A chronological resume puts emphasis on work experience. It is a good approach for candidates with steady work history where they can provide reverse chronological employment history, pointing out accomplishments in each position.

Functional Resume: This type of resume is focused on skills and accomplishments described at the beginning of the resume. It highlights key skills and accomplishments, pointing out what the candidate can do for the prospective employer. While this type of resume is desirable for entry level candidates and for some candidates with employment gaps, typically recruiters do not like this format. It makes it hard to determine what the candidate did in each of the previous jobs, and should only be used in cases where a chronological resume exposes weaknesses in the candidate's application.

Combination Resume: This is another possible approach that incorporates both chronological and functional formats. It can deliver the advantages of both types of resumes. It begins with a career summary, immediately following the header of the resume containing the name, address, phone number, and e-mail address. This enables you to state your qualifications, skills, and career summary at the beginning of the resume. You follow that with your employment history in a reverse chronological order. This format allows you to emphasize your skills and qualifications upfront while still providing the employment timeline the recruiters like to see. The addition of a career summary highlights the candidate's skills and qualifications so that the recruiter can easily determine if there is a possible match with job requirements. The combination resume is a good approach for candidates who want to make a major career change or re-enter the job market after a significant absence. This approach enables candidates to emphasize their skills and qualifications instead of work experience. Take care to keep it concise. A combination resume should not be any longer than either a chronological or functional resume.

CAREER SUMMARY

Career summary should be an effective declaration of your skills, accomplishments, and career goals. It is your career objective statement written in a way that will grab the employer's attention. It is a statement of what you can do, where you want to go, and how you can help your potential employer.

Here are some suggestions for preparing your career summary.

- **Research Your Ideal Position:** Before you start writing your career summary, you need to decide your career goals. What is your ideal job? Once you decide on the ideal position you are seeking, start reviewing the newspaper ads and job postings on the Internet. This will reveal the detailed position requirements and the qualifications desired by employers.
- **Determine Your Qualifications:** Compare the position requirements for your ideal job with your skills and qualifications. Do you have the needed skills? Do you meet the job requirements? Will you be able to help the prospective employer? What skills is the employer looking for? What special abilities do you possess which make you the perfect candidate? Do you have some personal strengths and qualities that will make you an asset for the prospective employer? Now prepare a detailed description of how your skills and qualifications meet the requirements for your ideal job.
- **Now Write a Summary:** Here, you need to emphasize how hiring you will help the employer. You need to show how the skills you possess, are transferable to your

next employer. Include your most important accomplishments and demonstrate how such accomplishments will help future employers. The focus of your summary should be on your greatest strengths and the major benefits you will bring to your new employer.

A resume must stand out as a good fit with job requirements. Hundreds of resumes are received by recruiters for every open position. More than 90% of resumes are discarded after a quick review. A recruiter's objective in reviewing resumes is to find candidates who will be able to handle the job responsibilities.

Resume Preparation

Your resume should state your qualifications in a concise and clear way. Any vague or incomplete statement or any error gets a resume thrown out quickly. The kind of resume you submit will determine whether you get invited for job interviews.

Fortunately, there are a lot of resources available to help you get your resume done right. Many of these resources are available to you at no cost. First and foremost is the help available on the Internet to write a resume. You may want to go to www.monster.com and www.careerbuilder.com to find some guidelines and help in preparing a resume.

You should get your resume critiqued by at least two professionals in your field. While comments of family members and friends can be helpful, there is no substitute for a critique by a professional in your field.

Ask yourself the following questions before writing your resume. Did I contribute to any project that increased profits for my employer? What was my role? How did it benefit my employer? Did I increase sales, revenue, or profits? Did I improve customer service? Did I increase production? Did I reduce employee turnover? You need to translate these benefits into tangible, quantifiable terms. This will enable you to show your prospective employers how you will be able to help them meet their goals.

Successful job applicants are those who tailor their resume and cover letter to a job posting. They keep in mind that recruiters are looking for candidates who match the job requirements. They carefully study a job posting and then submit a comparison of their skills and experience with job requirements.

Resume Building Blocks

Here are some building blocks for your resume.

- **Personal Information:** Full name, address, phone number and e-mail address should appear as header on the resume.
- **Target Job Title:** This should appear immediately after the personal information. You should pick a job title that appears most often in the job postings you have collected for your target job. This will help your resume to come up in database searches performed by recruiters.
- **Career Summary:** This should follow your target job title and describe what you are able to offer. This is just a couple of sentences that state what you can do and how you can help your employer. You should write your career summary before you prepare the rest of your resume. This will help you to decide what should be highlighted on your resume. Do not use general statements such as "seeking a challenging opportunity with a growing company". Such general statements are red flags that may cause recruiters to discard your re-

sume. The career summary should be related to the job for which you are submitting your resume. This is the first information on your resume following your name and address, and you need to make it highly effective.

- **Accomplishments:** A good description of your achievements will make your resume stand out in the big stack of resumes recruiters review every day. You should translate your achievements in monetary terms whenever possible. For example, if you are in sales, you should state how much revenue you were able to bring to your company. If you are in operations, you can state how much money you were able to save for your employer. By stating several achievements that helped your previous employers to make or save money, you increase your chances of being invited for employment interviews.

- **Unique Strengths:** You should think about your unique strengths and personal qualities, and develop a one sentence statement that describes the benefits you offer to prospective employers. This statement should be highlighted in your resume and cover letters.

- **Keywords:** Many companies now use keyword software to electronically scan resumes. That means you should make your resume scanner friendly by incorporating relevant keywords in your resume. To find the relevant keywords, you should study job postings for the positions of your interest. It is probable that the keywords in these postings are what the prospective employers will search for. Use those keywords that apply to the skills you possess. Sometimes good candidates are overlooked because keywords in the job posting are not included in the resume. Job postings are often a great place to identify the keywords that are important to a position. Such keywords appear in the responsibilities and job requirements portion of job postings. When you study job postings for several positions like the job you want, you will be able to develop a list of keywords to incorporate in your profile. Before sending your resume to an employer, make sure the keywords in the job posting are used in your resume and cover letter. The use of appropriate keywords is the most crucial element in getting your resume selected for further consideration.

- **Education and Training:** You should state in reverse chronological order the names of educational institutions, dates attended, major subjects, and degrees received. Include any special training.

- **Academic Awards and Honors:** Any awards, scholarships, honors, and special recognition you received as a student should be stated on the resume. Include any offices you held as a student and your contributions to sports, student publications, and other extra-curricular activities. This section is very important for entry level positions.

- **Work Experience:** Start with your current or most recent position and include prior work experience and accomplishments. Work experience should focus on the most recent jobs and describe the older jobs in lesser detail. You should include your position title, employer's name, location, and the employment dates. The order in which you want to present the job titles or company names depends on whether you want to emphasize the names of companies you worked for, or the positions you held. In addition to full time positions, you should feel free to include part-time jobs and volunteer work. Focus on the skills you developed and your achievements in each assignment. Any gaps in work history should be explained with short statements indicating what you were doing during that time. If you were home to raise children, engaged in part-time work or consulting projects, you should state that.

- **Skills:** Every job requires a specific set of skills to perform the job requirements. This includes transferable skills such as communication skills, interpersonal skills, leadership skills, planning skills and production skills. It includes job related skills also that are specific to an occupation. You need to describe each of your top skills in detail with examples of how you used those skills and the results you accomplished.

- **Country Specific Information:** While it is a common practice in some countries to include date of birth and marital status, such information should not be included on a resume in the United States. It is illegal in the US to discriminate in an employment decision based upon an applicant's age, sex, race, national origin, ethnic group, religion, or a physical disability. It is important to research local customs if you are applying for a job in another country.

- **Awards and Commendations:** If you have received awards or commendations from senior management of previous employers, be sure to include that information on your resume.

- **References:** You should not include names of your references on the resume. There is no need to say: "References available upon request". You are expected to have references. You should create a list of references and have it available to give at the interview or send by email as a follow-up.

Resume should not be longer than two pages. A one-page resume is quite appropriate for recent college graduates and to apply for entry level positions. On the other hand, persons with experience usually go to two pages. You should not staple a two-page resume. That makes it harder for the recipient to scan the resume or make photocopies. Remember to include your name and Page 2 on top of the second page of your resume.

A resume longer than two pages shows a lack of ability to communicate concisely. A longer resume does not demonstrate that a person has more experience than other candidates.

You should construct your resume from the viewpoint of employers. Respect the fact that resume reviewers typically review hundreds of resumes for each position. **You should do everything possible to answer the primary question in the recruiter's mind: "How will this candidate match our requirements?"** The more you can do to help answer that question, the closer you will be to getting the job.

Resume Check List

The following check list will help you to review the quality of your resume.

- Does it include a statement of career summary towards the top of the resume? Is this summary specific and related to your skills and qualifications?
- Have you included your accomplishments and quantified them?
- Have you checked and re-checked to ensure there are no spelling or grammatical errors? A single error could cause your resume to be discarded.
- Is it easy to understand the resume content?

- Have you included the appropriate keywords so that your resume will match job requirements when reviewed by a computer program?
- Does it include your work history with the most recent job listed first? Have you included a list of accomplishments?
- Does it have an attractive appearance with appropriate headings? Are the margins adequate and even? Is there consistent use of font size and spacing?
- Have you included your academic awards and honors?
- Have you labeled the resume sections?

Focus on your accomplishments. A resume should show how your employers benefited from your contributions. Explain your accomplishments clearly and concisely so that interviewers, who are not well versed in the technical aspects of your field, can still understand and appreciate your contributions.

Visual Resumes and Portfolios

Visual resume is an online resume that may include pictures and examples of your work. It is a graphical and visual approach to present your career objectives, job experience, accomplishments, skills, education, and other qualifications. It allows you to present yourself in ways beyond words on paper. It is an Internet based way to present the information included in traditional resumes. It presents information in a way that is visually more appealing. By using graphics and colors, visual resumes present the same information as the traditional resumes, but in a format that is more pleasing and stimulating. Some of the job search websites provide resume templates you can download. The purpose of a visual resume is to gain interviews just like the paper resume. Most employers prefer a traditional resume. However, for some jobs in creative industries like advertising and graphic design, a visual resume would be more desirable. It shows the candidate's creative abilities. You can go to the following websites to get additional information on visual resumes: www.monster.com www.topresume.com www.pinterest.com www.zety.com www.visualcv.com www.indeed.com

Video Resumes

Another new trend in resume preparation is the video resume. It is a way to demonstrate your communication skills and your personality. It allows employers to see and hear candidates and determine how they present themselves. It is not a substitute for the traditional resume, but another way to demonstrate your capabilities. It represents a video of personal qualifications developed by a candidate and placed on the Internet. The contents of a video resume are the same as the contents of a paper resume. It includes name, contact information, career objectives, educational background, special skills, and work experience. The suggested dress code for a video resume is the same as the dress code for a personal interview. When you are applying for a sales job or a job in the entertainment industry, a video resume will certainly help. Be sure that video resume presents you in a positive way and will enhance your image and appeal as a candidate. Practice many times before you record yourself; do not read from a script. Video resume should cover your key message in a conversational style, including your name, current position, unique qualifications, the position you are searching for, and why they should hire you. A video resume can make a powerful statement. It is a great way to present your communication skills and accomplishments and project a positive image. Some of the job-related websites have started accepting the online posting of video resumes. Video resumes will become more popular as our younger generation enters the workforce. Additional information on video resumes is available on various websites including: www.indeed.com, www.flexjobs.com, www.wyzowl.com, www.thebalancecareers.com

COVER LETTERS

A cover letter confirms that you have read the job posting, you understand the job requirements and you are really interested. It enables you to link your experience with the advertised job. And, it gives you the opportunity to provide any information specifically requested in the job posting that might not be included in your resume, such as job location preferences and availability date. A well prepared and tailor-made cover letter can be very helpful in your job search. It is a tool to draw attention to the most relevant information in the resume. Think of it as a requirement when you send a resume. Many recruiters do not even read resumes that come without cover letters.

Your cover letter is a sales pitch to a potential employer. It enables you to focus on those aspects of your qualifications that are particularly suited to an employer's needs. You should think of your cover letter as an advertisement. When you advertise a product or service, your focus is on selling that product or service. Similarly, in a cover letter, your focus is on selling yourself so that you will be invited for a job interview. A cover letter should be prepared specifically for each position. A generic cover letter is a mistake, and most recruiters spot it easily. The cover letter needs to be individually written to suit the circumstances of each situation.

You need to use your resume and cover letter in combination to sell yourself to prospective employers.

The appearance and content of the cover letter often determines whether the recruiter will review the resume. It also demonstrates a candidate's skill in written communication. It is an opportunity to show what you know about the position and how your qualifications match the job requirements.

To get a job in today's competitive market, you need to prepare a good resume and effective cover letters. It is much better to send your resume to a small number of targeted employers rather than doing a mass distribution. It is better to be qualitative rather than quantitative in approaching employers.

Cover Letter Objectives

A cover letter is generally written to meet one of the following needs:

- **To seek help in job search:** This is a networking letter sent to people you know who can help you in your job search. Such a letter is usually sent to friends, family members, social and professional contacts. The purpose of the letter is to get introductions to employers and recruiters, to find out about job openings, and to get job search advice from knowledgeable sources. You should put together an extensive list of your contacts, and then send them letters highlighting your skills and qualifications, the type of position you are seeking, and request help in making contacts. Remember to attach your resume with the networking letter. Always send a thank-you note to those who respond. And let your network know when you have found a job. It is important to keep your network active.

- **To inquire about job openings with employers:** This type of letter is sent to the hiring managers to inquire about possible job openings that may match your skills and qualifications. While such letters are not in response to specific job postings, you still need to explain how your qualifications would match the company's requirements. That means, you still need to research the employer to whom you are sending your cover letter and resume. Your letter should state how you plan to follow-up with the employer.

- **To inquire about executive search assignments**: The purpose of such letters is to find out if the executive search firm has an assignment that could be a good match with your background and qualifications. These letters are like the letters you may send to companies to inquire about job openings. An important difference is that you need to spell out your salary requirements and job preferences in detail to executive recruiters. You need to let the recruiters know about your geographic preferences, the type of industry and position you are looking for, your current salary and the salary range you are willing to consider for a new position. You should be very specific. Recruiters receive hundreds of resumes each day, and they pay attention to only those candidates they think they can place with a client organization. You need to be very frank with the recruiter. Any attempt to withhold requested information is not a good approach for working with executive recruiters.

- **To apply in response to ads and job postings:** This is the type of cover letter used most frequently. When you find a job advertisement that matches your qualifications and interest, you need to prepare an appropriate cover letter to submit with your resume.

Each job has different needs and requirements, and you want to highlight the relevant skills and qualifications in your letter. Therefore, you need to write a separate cover letter in response to each job posting. One way to accomplish this is to prepare a detailed list of the positions you have held, experiences, skills, accomplishments, awards and honors, education, and other qualifications. Then you can pick those qualifications that are most relevant to a job posting, and highlight them in your cover letter.

Cover Letter Preparation

You must review the job requirements before preparing a cover letter. Job requirements are usually included in job postings and newspaper ads. You should read this information a couple of times to be sure that your skills and qualifications match what the job requires. It is a good sign when you find that your qualifications match most of the requirements. This means, you are a strong candidate for the position. Next, you should underline the primary responsibilities indicated in the job posting, and write down the strongest qualifications you possess to match what the job requires. This is what you want to highlight in your cover letter.

A cover letter should fit in one page with ample margins. It should contain three to four paragraphs. You should begin with a strong statement describing how you heard about the job opening and the reasons for your interest. This is also the place to explain any prior contacts with the company, such as a phone conversation, or if the candidate is being referred by someone known to the employer. The cover letter should explain what you know about the position and the company, and how your skills and experiences match what the employer needs. You should not say how the job will benefit you. Instead, the emphasis should always be on how you will benefit the company.

A cover letter should include the date, the recipient's name, title, company name and address and a personalized salutation. The body of the letter should include a statement indicating your interest in the position (including any identifier mentioned in the job posting) and where you saw the posting. If you are sending your letter and resume as a follow-up on a phone conversation or as a referral from someone known to the employer, you should state that in the first paragraph. The second paragraph should describe how your qualifications match the job requirements. A possible approach is to state the job requirements and then highlight how you fit those requirements. Here you should make a reference to your resume for additional information. You can end the letter by thanking the reader, and indicating the next step. You can say that you look forward to hearing from the employer, and be sure to include your phone number and e-mail address where you can be reached. As an alternative, you can mention your intent to follow-up with a phone call. This is a good way to show your enthusiasm and strong interest, and often gives you the opportunity to learn more about the position and the company when you make the follow-up call.

Cover letter is an opportunity for you to differentiate yourself from other candidates. You can do so by highlighting how your skills and experiences will benefit the employer. A good cover letter will persuade the employer to call you for an interview.

Cover Letter Tips

Here are some tips for preparing your cover letters.

- **Address the letter to a person:** Your letter will be far more effective if it is addressed by name to the person doing the hiring. You should devote the needed time and effort to find out the name and title of the hiring manager. If this information is not included in the job posting, you can often find it on the Internet or by calling the company's main office. Once you have this information, you should use a formal salutation such as Dr., Mr., or Ms. to address your cover letter. You should not begin a cover letter with Dear Sir or Madam, or address it To Whom It May Concern. The use of generic salutations in cover letters shows lack of real interest in the opportunity.
- **Mention prior contact:** When you are following up on a phone conversation or a prior meeting, always mention that at the beginning of your cover letter to remind the reader.
- **Never use a form letter:** Recruiters can quickly tell the difference between a form letter and the one designed specifically to meet the requirements of a job opening. Resumes attached to form letters are often ignored by recruiters. When you are really interested in the job opening, take the time to prepare a cover letter that highlights your skills and experiences as they relate to the job requirements.
- **Keep it short:** A cover letter should not be more than one page. It should be organized in just a few paragraphs to highlight your suitability for the job opening. Do not repeat what is already stated in the resume. A cover letter is intended to spark the reader's interest to review your resume and should offer something more than what is contained in the resume.

- **Research the company:** The quality of your cover letter will depend on how much you know about the company. You should visit the company's website and review trade publications to find out about the company's mission, values, history, current customers and operating results. This information will also help you when you interview with the company.
- **Explain how you meet the job requirements:** You need to highlight an understanding of the job requirements and how your skills and experiences match those requirements. You should include examples of your accomplishments in similar roles in prior positions.
- **State the next step**: Remember to state how you will follow-up. If it is your intention to call the employer in a week to request an interview, you should state that in the letter. And, make it a point to put that on your calendar and then do it.
- **Letter should appear professional:** The letter should include your name and contact information as well as the name, title, company name and full address of the hiring manager. The letter should appear attractive, and make sure there are no typographical or grammatical errors. You should use a spell checker. In addition, proofread several times and have someone else proofread it for you. This is your first impression to the hiring company, and you certainly want to make it a good impression.

The quality of the cover letter often determines whether it opens the door for an interview. You need to devote as much attention to preparing the cover letters as you do to preparing your resume. A cover letter is what the recruiter will see even before glancing at your resume. It is the first impression of a candidate to a prospective employer. If this impression is not favorable, the resume is likely to be discarded.

You should never mention salary in your cover letters unless you are communicating with an executive search firm. Those matters will come up for discussion when the employer has decided to make you an offer. Any mention of compensation issues by the candidate prior to that is untimely.

Each cover letter must be tailor-made for each position in which you are interested. You should carefully review the position requirements stated in the job posting. You should write down your relevant qualifications next to each requirement. Your cover letter is essentially a summary of how your skills and experiences fit the job requirements. If you possess the needed qualifications, and you communicate that in your cover letter, it is probable that you will be called for an interview. You can review some sample cover letters by going to the various job search websites.

Email Cover Letters

The strategy for preparing an electronic cover letter is the same as for preparing a cover letter to be sent by regular mail. You need to demonstrate how your qualifications meet the requirements listed in the job posting.

There are some elements that differentiate e-mail cover letters. You need to provide all the information you would include in a printed cover letter, and you need to do that in fewer words and lesser space. Make sure to list those qualifications and experiences that match the job requirements. Your e-mail is a selling document, and you should make it highly effective. You should state the purpose of your e-mail in the subject line. This subject line should be attractive enough to cause the recipient to open your e-mail message. Remember to include your resume as an attachment with the e-mail message, and name your resume document something other than Resume. doc. Including your name in the filename of your document will help the recruiter to save your application for future reference. Never use the employer's name or the recruiter's name as the file name for your resume. I was amazed at the large number of resumes I received as a recruiter using my name or my search firm's name as the file name for the resume. It was hard to retrieve such resumes from my database unless I changed the file names before storing such resumes.

Another difference between e-mail and hard copy cover letter is the format. Your address and contact information goes below your name in e-mail while such information appears at the top in a hard copy cover letter.

When you need additional help for preparing your resume, just type the word "resume" on Google or another search engine. There is a lot of useful information available on the Internet at no cost.

CHAPTER 5

CONNECTING WITH EMPLOYERS

Every strike brings me closer to the next home run.
                                        —Babe Ruth

Once you have prepared a resume and online profiles that show your skills and abilities, the next step is to make sure that you come to the attention of those who are responsible for hiring.

The Covid-19 pandemic has changed how to connect with employers. Many jobs have switched to remote work and are likely to stay that way. When connecting with employers for remote wok, you need to demonstrate your ability and experience in working from home. This may include description of previous jobs which required working from home. You may want to mention your experience with high speed internet and the ability to handle video equipment.

Posting your resume on one or more job-boards is not enough. You need to find and actively approach many potential employers to find a suitable job. There is no one source for jobs that will lead you to a position well matched with your skills and job interests. You should make use of several sources of finding potential employers to complete a successful job search.

The following are major sources for locating potential employers who may have positions that suit your career objectives and requirements:

- Targeting companies of special interest to you
- Networking through business contacts, family, and friends
- Executive search firms and employment agencies
- Job postings on the Internet
- Job fairs and virtual career fairs

It is a good idea to use three to four available sources to locate suitable job openings. Your objective in contacting potential employers is to get interviews. Track those sources which generate more interviews for you, and devote greater effort to those sources, but continue to use more than one source for job search.

You are putting yourself at a disadvantage when you apply only for advertised job openings. Not only you will be competing against a very large number of candidates who apply for advertised jobs, you will be ignoring a vast number of jobs that are filled without ever being advertised. You should spend no more than 50% of your time on advertised job openings. More than 50% of your time should be devoted to your target list of employers; researching these companies, and using your network to develop contacts with people at your target employers.

The two most effective methods of job search are: making direct contact with the targeted companies of special interest to you, and networking through your business associates, friends, relatives and other contacts. These two methods lead to jobs that have not been advertised or posted on the Internet. Targeting companies and networking are two ways to tap this hidden job market.

Targeting Companies

Targeting companies of special interest to you is the most effective strategy for job search. This is particularly true when you are looking for a senior level position. This strategy begins with research into your target industry, and leads to the identification of companies that interest you based on size, growth potential, location and other factors important to you.

You will need to regularly update your target list based on research and your contacts with these companies. This process will also yield information about the names and titles of persons you need to approach in each company. You can find a list of companies by going to the yellow pages of the local phone directories, business directories available in public libraries, as well as online directories. Once you have a list of potential employers, you can research them by going to the employer websites, reading company annual reports, and searching for profiles of employers such as those available at www.hoovers.com. Some of the online business directories also include links to company websites. Another element in this research is to go to a search engine such as www.google.com and find additional information about the company's products, customers, and senior officers, which will enable you to network your way into those companies, or make direct contact with hiring managers. This approach requires a clear understanding of your own skills and interests, and the ability to conduct research of possible employers. It requires deciding what kind of companies to research, what to look for, and how to prioritize the companies you have picked.

Researching companies is critical when you are searching for a job. It can help you to focus on companies that fit your career goals. You can research companies by going to their websites. That will tell you about the company products and services, the markets they serve, the company size and location, how long they have been in business, their mission statement, the names of senior officers, and the company finances. You can research the company further by reading their press releases and news stories. Another excellent resource is the company annual report. You can find it online and that will give you a good overview of their operations.

When you have researched your target companies, you will know their operations, and the type of opportunities available with them that match your skills and experiences. You should send a personalized letter to the hiring manager at each company explaining how your background and experiences match the company's requirements, and attach a copy of your resume. You should state in your letter when you will call the hiring manager to set up an appointment for interview. In addition to approaching target companies by mail, you could call the hiring manager on the phone, briefly describe your qualifications and job interest, and try to get an appointment for a face-to-face interview. Remember to prepare a written outline of what you are going to say before you make that phone call. You should be able to set up some job interviews using this approach. Another possible approach is to go to the employer location, and try to meet with the hiring manager without an appointment. If you are not able to see the hiring manager, try to get a date and time when you could come back for an interview. If you are told there are no job openings, express your interest in future vacancies, and still try to get an interview. A personal visit to the job location can help you to establish contacts. Also, this is an opportunity to pick up some literature about the employer that could help you when you come back for an interview.

While large companies remain excellent places to work, many small to medium size companies are offering wonderful career opportunities.

Small companies give you the opportunity to be a big fish in a small pond. You can have broader responsibility and more impact on the company's operation in a short time. When preparing a list of your target companies, do not limit yourself to just large corporations. There is often big opportunity in small companies. If you are planning to target small companies, you can often find opportunities by contacting venture capital firms, private equity firms, small business services, and corporate attorneys who maintain a roster of small to medium sized clients. By going to people who work closely with smaller companies, you can often get a warm introduction into several companies. Many firms that work with small and medium businesses are happy to make introductions to senior management at their client companies because it demonstrates additional value that they provide. Some small companies and start-ups offer huge compensation packages. Be careful and evaluate that the company has the resources to honor such commitments.

Targeting companies of special interest is the most effective job search method. But it does not always lead to a successful job search for all candidates. You must plan to use three to four different job search methods for successful completion of your job search.

Networking

This approach involves contacting the people you know to put you in touch with potential employers and to introduce you to additional contacts who might be able to provide similar help.

While face-to-face networking is not desirable during the pandemic, you should consider shifting your focus to online efforts. Join groups on LinkedIn in your field and participate by making comments and sharing articles. Search for companies you would like to work for, and look out for any job openings that

match your profile. Subscribe to any blogs or newsletters that interest you.

The starting point in networking is to develop a comprehensive list of your contacts including friends, former employers, clients, vendors at previous employers, business associates, family members, former teachers, neighbors, members of professional associations you belong to, and people from your religious groups and community groups. Your network should consist of these people as well as of the people they know. Your goal should be to select contacts with some knowledge about the type of work you desire, and those who are likely to know others who could help you in your job search.

Actively networking with people in your industry is the most important step in job search. This requires initiative, and at the same time, a diplomatic way to approach your contacts. You don't want to come across as someone desperate for a job. You need to position yourself as a problem solver who is trying to gather information to evaluate whether a company is the right fit. You want to be on a learning mission to determine if your skills and interests match what the company needs.

To overcome feelings of awkwardness, you may want to start with family members and friends. Once you are comfortable working with friends, you can start reaching out to a wider circle. Start out with people who have jobs similar to the job you are seeking. Try to gain knowledge about their jobs and industry, and find out if they are aware of any open positions. You don't want to appear imposing or aggressive. People want to help others and a soft approach will take you a long way.

Your contacts must believe that you are a good candidate with the skills, knowledge and experience required for the type of job in which you are interested. Unless your contacts like you and believe in your credentials, they will be reluctant to refer you to others for possible opportunities. The quality of approach you make to your contacts is very important. You need to come across as someone highly accomplished, and at the same time, you do not want to appear pushy at any time. You should prepare an outline of what you want to say before you make a phone call. The essential question you need to ask your contacts is this: Do you know of any job openings suitable for me at your place of work or somewhere else? If the answer is no, you should ask a follow-up question: Do you know someone who could help me in my job search? If you can do that successfully, you will get good leads for job openings, and gain additional contacts who could lead you to the job you desire.

Many people feel shy about making use of their contacts to do job hunting, and therefore, networking is not used as widely as it should be. This is a highly effective way of finding unadvertised positions, particularly for senior level positions. You should dedicate a substantial part of your job search effort to networking. You simply start telling the people you know that you are looking for a job, and the type of job you are looking for. These people may be able to introduce you to other people, who may be able to help you find a job. When you have created your target list of companies, let your network know about it, and ask them if they know any contacts in those companies or they could refer you to others for possible contacts in those companies.

Networking is one of the most effective ways to find a job, and you are very well positioned whenever you are being referred by an employee within the company.

Most people you contact will not be able to help you immediately. But some will know of job openings in your field, or know of someone who works in your field who could help you. Networking means contacting people you know, and reaching out to people you do not know. This involves cultivating relationships, and making those relationships useful for the persons in your network. Develop a habit of building your contact information, and use your network to develop additional contacts. The information you collect about your network contacts should include the name, phone number, employer's name, position, educational background, special interests and any other information that will be helpful in cultivating relationships.

The Internet has opened new possibilities for networking.

Social networks have become an important resource for job-hunters. LinkedIn is a popular social network with a relationship-powered job network that connects job applicants with hiring managers and recruiters. LinkedIn is the world's largest professional network. It is a place to connect with people you have known in the past, and build new connections. It also has a customized URL feature that allows you to have a personalized URL you can use in your correspondence. For instance, my URL is www.linkedin.com/in/NarinderMehta. It is not enough to have a LinkedIn account. You need a complete profile that includes your professional capabilities and points out why the recruiters should talk to you. You can also post your picture, and you should certainly do that. LinkedIn is available as a free service. You can also get premier membership which provides additional benefits for a fee.

In addition to finding job listings on LinkedIn, candidates get background information on the job posters that can help them to prepare targeted cover letters. LinkedIn also helps candidates to identify their contacts who can refer them to the hiring manager or to someone who knows the hiring manager. Additional information is available on the website www.linkedin.com.

Facebook is the world's largest social network that enables people to stay connected with friends and family, find out what is happening in the world, and to share their thoughts. It is a wonderful place to check for updates by your contacts and share messages. It is becoming a good place to look for job opportunities. Facebook has a section called the Marketplace where you can list anything you want such as the job you are looking to land. You can join Facebook groups that cater to your career interests and post comments. You can search for information on jobs and careers by going to www.facebook.com/jobhunting.

Remember not to post anything on Facebook and other social media websites that you don't want your current employer or prospective employers to see. Comments or photos that are not appropriate can cost you a job offer. Many candidates are turned down for good jobs because of improper posts on Facebook and other websites. Employers scan social media profiles to evaluate candidates. Any negative comments about a previous boss or employer, discriminatory comments related to race, religion, or gender will work against you. On the other hand, any positive aspects of your profile will help you when recruiters scan social media. You should work on building a strong social profile. When you are looking for work, share updates about your job search with your Facebook community.

While LinkedIn is focused on professional networking, Facebook is a place to connect with family and friends, Twitter is a place where people express opinions and build relations. Twitter is a social networking site that allows users to send micro-messages of 140 characters or less. You can post your own tweets or read tweets of other people by following them. Go to www.twitter.com. Hashtags on Twitter are search terms used in tweets and identified by a preceding pound sign. You can use hashtags to find information about career opportunities and information related to your profession. You can find your information on your target companies by going to Twitter. It has also become a place to search for connections that may lead to job opportunities.

Also remember that expanding your network need not be limited to face-to-face events. Authoring a blog can be a great way to build your personal brand, expand your network of business contacts, and demonstrate your knowledge and skills to employers.

Maintain a complete record of your network contacts, send thank-you notes whenever they help you, and remember to let them know when you accept a new position. While networking is the second most effective way to find a job, it is estimated that only about one-third of the candidates who rely upon networking alone to find a job will be successful. Once again, this points out how important it is to use several methods to find a job.

Executive Search Firms

Executive recruiters or headhunters as they are more commonly known, work from outside the hiring company to attract management talent.

Headhunters advertise jobs, interview candidates, and present suitable candidates for final decision to be made by the employer. They have access to senior management jobs around the world. They determine which candidates are to be introduced to client organizations. The employers hire search firms to find special talent which is in short supply. Executive recruiters look for candidates who are currently employed, have a good growth record, and are making good compensation.

Headhunters can be very helpful to you at some time in your career. It is wise to cultivate relationships with some of them in your field. When you have the background and qualifications of interest to a search firm, you will get immediate attention. On the other hand, remember that search firms work for employers and get paid by them. When you do not get a response from a search firm, it means that you do not meet the criteria for the positions they are trying to fill. It does not in any way reflect upon your ability and qualifications. It just means that the search firm you contacted is not focused on finding candidates for positions you can fill.

There are two types of executive search firms: retained search firms and contingency search firms. Retained search firms generally have an exclusive assignment to fill a specific position, and they get their fee even if they are not able to fill the position. Contingency search firms are paid a fee only when they fill a position.

The starting point for your approach to executive search firms is to realize that they are not under any obligation to talk to you. Their fees and expenses are paid by hiring companies, and their primary obligation is to the employers. However, they need suitable candidates to meet their obligation to client organizations. A recruiter from a search firm would be interested in talking to you only when you are a good match for a current search assignment, a possible match for a future assignment, or when you are referred by a good source known to the search firm.

The search firms receive hundreds of resumes for each job posting. They go through a quick screening to find possible candidates. As a recruiter, I could find only one or two suitable candidates for phone interviews, out of every 100 resumes I received. The other applicants did not fit my area of recruiting specialization, lacked the required qualifications, or just did not generate any interest for further investigation.

Whenever sending your resume to a search firm, remember to include a cover note pointing out how you fit the job requirements for an advertised position or the search firm's area of specialization.
When you are contacted by an executive search firm, you should expect to answer questions about your background, experience, and current compensation. The recruiter is trying to determine whether to consider you for referral to the client organization. Any attempt to withhold information or provide a vague answer is likely to disqualify you from further consideration.

When the headhunter considers you a possible match with the job requirements, you will probably have a phone interview to be followed by face-to-face interviews. And when the recruiter decides to refer you to the hiring company, you will be invited for interviews with the employer. Since the executive search firms are paid by hiring companies, they always try to satisfy the employer's interest. **The employers pay substantial search fees for recruiting candidates through executive search firms, and they use this resource mostly for senior management positions or those positions that are hard to fill.** Retained search firms generally charge a fee of 1/3 of the first year's compensation; fees of contingency search firms generally fall in the range of 20% to one-third of the first year's salary. Reliance upon executive search firms is more useful for candidates for senior level positions and less effective for junior level jobs.

Job Postings on the Internet

Job postings on the Internet are becoming an increasingly important way for companies to bring their open positions to the attention of candidates.

In addition to placing open positions on their own websites, the employers use a wide variety of job boards such as www.monster.com, www.careerbuilder.com, www.ziprecruiter.com, www.craigslist.org, and other websites for specific industries or professions. A list of job board websites is included in Chapter 3 Using the Internet Resources.

When you are searching on the Internet, you can tailor your job search by using the following criteria:

- Location: Select your location unless you are open to relocation
- Industry: Select the industry in which you want to work
- Job Category: Choose the most relevant job category

Your resume should include keywords generally used in the category of jobs for which you are applying. Most employers use applicant tracking systems to limit the number of resumes selected for consideration.

The Internet can do a wonderful job of connecting a candidate with a potential employer in a very short time. Many job postings on the Internet are blind ads without employer identification. Employers do not want to handle phone calls, and therefore, they post jobs without identifying themselves. Your resume and cover letter determine how you are evaluated. Employers are always flooded with resumes, and candidates are always fighting a numbers game when they try to find a job on the Internet. A strong candidate, who responds quickly with a targeted cover letter and resume, has a better chance of making the short list of candidates invited for interview.

Whenever an e-mail address is given in the job posting by an employer, send your resume by e-mail. Include a cover note referencing the job posting and highlight how you match the job requirements. You should follow-up the e-mailed resume by sending a hard copy of the resume and a tailor-made cover letter. This enables you to get a well prepared and formatted resume and cover letter in the employer's hands. This may give you an edge as most other candidates will just e-mail their resumes.

Cover letters are extremely important when responding to job postings on the Internet. You should gather all the available information, and then prepare a letter focused on the employer needs and how your qualifications match those needs. An effective way is to mention the job requirements and highlight how your qualifications match what is required. Whenever possible, you should address your letter to the hiring manager by name. If a name is not included in the ad, you should try to find it by calling the company's office.

You should make a follow-up call, within a week after sending a resume, to confirm that the resume has been received and to see if you can schedule an appointment for a phone interview or a face-to-face interview. This is also an opportunity for you to get the full job description and other information about the hiring company.

You should not rely upon the Internet exclusively for your job search. You will find much greater success in job search when you combine the use of the Internet with heavy focus on target companies of special interest to you as well as use of networking.

Job Fairs

Job fairs provide a way to explore possible job opportunities and to learn about the companies that are actively hiring.

There is a variety of job fairs: on-campus job fairs for college students; commercial job fairs for professional occupations; specialty job fairs focused on specialty groups such as computers; and general purpose job fairs representing a wide range of industries and occupations.

Job fairs present networking opportunities with employer representatives and with other attendees. When you enter a job fair, your priority should be to get a list of participating employers and job openings available with them. You should focus just on those companies that fit your job interests. Some attendees tend to go from booth to booth, and that is unproductive. Also, there is a lot of information available on the employer organizations which can be helpful in identifying your target organizations and preparing for interviews.

Your focus during the job fair should be on collecting information, developing contacts, and to see if you can lay the ground work to schedule an interview. This is a good place to gather business cards and make notes that will be helpful in the job search process. You should make detailed notes while your interactions at the job fair are still fresh in your mind. Follow-up with the contacts you established at the job fair by sending thank-you notes and copies of your resume. Attending job fairs is just one step in the job search process, and you should not be disappointed if it does not translate into job interviews.

Virtual career fair is a new twist on job fairs. Recruiters and candidates meet in a virtual space. It is an interactive online experience that connects candidates with employers. Recruiters meet candidates online, and candidates share their information with companies that are hiring. Some employers sponsor their own virtual career fairs and others are organized by associations. Such fairs save employers time and money and broaden the candidate pool available to them. When candidates log into a virtual fair, they can access "booths" arranged by job field or company name. When they access a booth, they will find information about the company and the jobs available. Sometimes they are also able to have conversations with recruiters and hiring managers. You can find information about job fairs on social networking services such as LinkedIn and Facebook. Anyone interested in attending the trade show can do so free of charge. There is no travel involved. The only place the candidates need to go is in front of their computers. The purpose of such fairs is to generate interest among candidates. Suitable candidates, found through job fairs, are invited by employers for face-to-face interviews.

How Employers Fill Positions

Human capital is the most important resource for any company's growth.

Take a careful look at how a company handles human resources, and you will know how successful that company will be in the long run. When a company has done a good job of finding employees, and they are motivated towards building the company, the sky is the limit for its growth. If the company has a haphazard hiring process or the employees are not happy, the company will eventually fall apart.

The most desirable way for an employer to fill a position is to do so from within the organization. Employers like to hire persons whose work they have seen. If you really want to work for a company, and you cannot get hired in the job you want, try working for them part-time or as an independent contractor or consultant. That is one way to build a career with the company you really want to work for.

There are two ways employers use to find new employees. They do the recruiting on their own, or use outside resources for recruiting such as executive search firms and employment agencies.

1. **Direct recruiting by employers:** Most companies employ internal recruiters. They are company employees and are paid a salary just like other employees. They have job titles such as "Recruiter" or "Hiring Specialist". Their primary role is to identify candidates who meet job requirements for designated positions. Employers may post jobs on one or more job boards on the Internet, place employment ads in newspapers and trade journals, and post the job on company website and bulletin boards. As a result, they receive hundreds of resumes for each job posting. Their approach is to first screen out candidates to come up with a manageable number for interviews. A few candidates who make it through the screening process are invited for face-to-face interviews. Two or three of these candidates will get invited for follow-up interviews, and one of them may receive a job offer to work for the company. The selected candidate will be offered an employment package consisting of salary, bonus, benefits, and relocation assistance when needed.

2. **Recruiting through outside sources:** Employers also use outside sources such as, executive search firms and employment agencies to attract suitable talent. The outside sources charge fees from employers for finding suitable candidates. External recruiters can be classified based on their compensation arrangement. There are two main models: contingency fee and retainer search. A recruiter who works on a contingency fee basis gets paid when a candidate accepts the job offer and reports to work. If the position is filled through internal efforts or through another source, the contingency recruiter does not get paid. Retained search firms work on an exclusive basis. Only one firm is given the assignment

to find and present candidates. They work closely with the hiring department of a company to develop and execute a strategy to find suitable candidates. Retainer search is mostly used for senior level positions and technical positions that are hard to fill. **I founded and managed an executive search firm for ten years, and worked with many employers.** I charged a fee equal to 25% of the first year's salary of a placed employee; most recruiters charge a fee in the range of 20% to one-third of the first year's salary. The employers are willing to pay substantial executive search fees to find exceptional employees. To attract candidates for my search assignments, I made extensive use of my network of contacts in the industry to identify suitable candidates. I would share the details of my search assignments with my network and seek their recommendations regarding exceptional candidates. In addition, I would place job postings on my own website as well as on major job boards, and place ads in trade journals. I would conduct extensive interviews with candidates and talk to some of their references. I would generally select two to three candidates for consideration by the client organization. The hiring decision was up to the employer. When the employer decided to offer the job to a candidate I submitted, I would play the role of an intermediary to come up with an employment package acceptable to the candidate. This involved coordination of negotiations between the employer and the candidate regarding the base salary, bonus arrangements, and relocation assistance.

To find the job you deserve, you must target the employers of special interest to you, focus on your

network, and use other job search methods available to you. You should not limit yourself to just one method of job search. When you focus on just one source for jobs, you are limiting your chances of a successful job search. The candidates who use just one method of job search are likely to get frustrated, and some of them will abandon their job search. It is a good idea to use three to four available sources to connect with potential employers.

CHAPTER 6

INTERVIEWING FOR JOBS

When I am getting ready to reason with a man, I spend one-third of my time thinking about myself and what I am going to say and two-thirds about him and what he is going to say.

—Abraham Lincoln

This chapter is designed to help you: prepare for interviews, perform well during the interview process, and to follow-up after the interview. Job offers do not necessarily go to candidates who will do the best job. Often the jobs are offered to those who present themselves in the best way during the interview process.

Your interview objective should be to prove that you are the best candidate for the job; coming up as the second best is not enough.

The pandemic has radically changed the workplace. Many employers that were entirely in-office have shifted to working remotely. Some are having to build new teams remotely. Many companies are working remotely for the first time, hiring remotely for the first time, and some are onboarding remotely for the first time.

Finding a job now is harder than it was in the pre-pandemic days. It may take longer to get a response, schedule an interview, and get a job offer. But you can still differentiate yourself from the crowd by developing an understanding of the recruiting process and how the pandemic has changed it. You should create a good personal impression, communicate effectively how your skills and experiences match the job requirements, and then follow-up after the interview.

VIRTUAL INTERVIEWS

Because of Covid-19, most employers have shifted to virtual interviews. These interviews take place remotely, sometimes by use of phone, but often using videoconferencing technology such as Zoom, Google Hangouts, Microsoft Teams and Skype. Such interviews allow direct communication and recordable interviews that can be accessed by others. This approach also helps to reduce the expense of bringing candidates from out of town for face-to-face interviews.

Virtual interviews follow the format of traditional face-to-face interviews, but there are some additional considerations for candidates. Such an interview requires a computer with camera and microphone, a downloaded software such as Zoom, and an internet connection. You should prepare for the interview just as you would for a face-to-face interview. This includes researching the company, carefully checking the job description and identifying how your skills match what is required. You need to check your equipment for use in the video interview, and check to be sure that you will be able to log on to the employer's video conferencing network.

Virtual interviewing is new for many companies and they are navigating their way. For most job hunters, virtual interviewing is something they have not done before. It is new and different. Although virtual interviewing is done online, you should prepare for it just as you would prepare for an in-person interview. Even though the interview is taking place from your home, you should expect it to be as formal as an interview at the employer's office. Your goal should be to come across as a suitable candidate who meets the job requirements and deserves further consideration for the position.

Here are some tips to help you prepare for virtual interviews:

- **Check the equipment:** When your virtual interview is confirmed, make sure to check all aspects of the equipment you will use. This includes the camera, microphone, headphone, video screen, internet connection, and software program for the interview (Zoom, Google Hangouts, Microsoft Teams, Skype). Plan to do the video interview on a laptop or desk top computer instead of a mobile phone. Technical ability is important in most jobs, and you don't want to come across as lacking in this skill. Check your equipment again on the day of the interview. Plan to keep the camera at an eye level and focus on the camera while you are talking.

- **Check what the interviewer will see:** You want to make sure that your background is neat and tidy. You don't want clutter in the background. The area you will be sitting in should be well lit. It is a good idea to plan to sit in front of a book shelf with some books you have read on display. Let people in your household know about the interview timing so that there will not be any distractions or interruptions. Silence your cell phone. Make sure there are no other phones in the room that may start ringing. Your personal appearance in a video interview is very important. Plan to dress just as you would for a face-to-face interview. Business attire will give you a sense of confidence and help you come across as a professional.

- **Do your homework:** Preparation is the key to success in a virtual interview, just as it is in a traditional interview. You should be ready to answer questions just as you would in in-person interviews. You need to research the company and the job. It is a good idea to visit the company's website, learn their history, products and services. You should plan to do a Google search to read the recent press releases and news stories. You should review the job description and identify how your skills and background match the job requirements. Talk to some current and former employees, and do some research on Glassdoor and other websites. You should review the interviewer's profile on LinkedIn to find out some areas of common interest.

- **Anticipate interview questions:** You should put together a list of questions you are likely to be asked and prepare your answers. Review a list of common questions included in this chapter. In addition, there will be questions related to the job and its responsibilities. Be prepared to answer some behavioral questions that are designed to determine how you behaved in specific situations. The interviewer is trying to determine how you reacted in real life situations and what value you added. Such questions are based on the concept that a person's past performance is the best predictor of future performance. You should also prepare a list of questions you want to ask. The interview is a two-way process. The employer is trying to determine if you are the most suitable candidate for the job, and you are there to determine if this is the right place to build your career. You should rehearse the interview with a friend or family member or in front of a mirror. You can also video tape an interview to see how you perform and what improvements are needed.

- **Connect with the interviewer:** Your goal should be to build a rapport with the interviewer. When you are well prepared, it will be easier for you to build a connection with the interviewer. Focus not only on what you are going to say, but how you are going to say it. Plan on talking slowly with emphasis on your main points so that what you say will have an impact. A recruiter sees many candidates each day. You want to create a lasting impression and be remembered. Plan to tell a personal story the recruiter is likely to remember. Be courteous, and carefully listen to each question. If you don't understand a question, politely ask the interviewer to repeat it. Do not interrupt, and if you both happen to be speaking at the same time, apologize and let the interviewer continue. Your goal is to demonstrate that you are the best candidate for the job. To accomplish that, you need to demonstrate how you match the job requirements and how you will be a good member of the team.

- **Follow-up after the interview:** This is critical. You should always send a thank-you note. It is not only polite, it is essential to create a good impression. This is an opportunity to highlight how you match what the job requires, and express your interest in becoming a member of the team. Also plan to prepare a written summary after the interview. That will be very helpful to you in subsequent interviews with this employer.

While virtual interviews are new and different, they do offer some advantages. Switching to virtual interviews saves time and provides flexibility for the interviewers as well as candidates. But the purpose of the interview has not changed. It is still the process to find the best candidates. Because the in-person link is missing in virtual interviews, there is often the need for additional interviews. You may be asked to appear for more interviews and to give virtual presentations.

INTERVIEWS WITHOUT INTERVIEWERS

Because of the pandemic, we are seeing the emergence and growth of interviews without any interviewers. Instead of speaking to a recruiter on the phone or by video chat, the job applicants are being asked to record their answers to questions about their job experience, skills, and personal qualities. Some applicants are also being asked to complete online tests to measure their abilities and personal traits. The employers can evaluate a larger number of applicants by relying on videos. Recorded video answers reduce the hiring bias by asking the same questions, and in the same format, from all applicants. Job seekers can answer video questions at their own convenience rather than having to meet an interviewer's schedule. Video recorded interviews can be done after work hours and on the week-ends. The pandemic has accelerated the use of digital hiring systems. New ways of assessing applicants have started to emerge. Pymetrics, a US based firm, has developed games to assess candidate personality traits to develop pools of high performing candidates.

PANDEMIC RELATED QUESTIONS

You are likely to be asked some questions about the pandemic when you appear for an interview. Here are some questions that are likely to come up.

- *Did you have to start working from home and what adjustments were needed?* Most workers had to start working from home for the first time. Explain how you separated your work life. Discuss if you had to set up a separate work area with the needed computer and other equipment. Highlight how you achieved results just as good or better than the results you were getting while working from office. Point out what working hours you maintained to ensure good production.

- *Can you tell me how the pandemic has affected your career?* If you were laid off, explain what steps you took to upgrade your skills. If the working hours were reduced, point out how you used the available time. This is an opportunity to explain how you organized your daily activities to search for a new job.

- *How do you manage your day when working remotely?* Tell the recruiter how you have managed your work day to achieve superior results. Explain the work schedule you have maintained and how you separated your work life from home activities.

- *How do you communicate while working from home?* Describe your use of Zoom, phone connections, and email. Explain how you have maintained regular communications with clients, vendors, and co-workers.

- *What are the lessons you learned during the pandemic?* You may want to explain what you learned about yourself while working remotely. Mention what are your preferred hours of work and how you follow through. This is an opportunity to share some stories of exceptional results you accomplished while working remotely.

- *Would you like to return to work from a traditional office?* Tell them how you feel about working from an office as compared to working remotely. Point out any concerns you have about working from a traditional office until the pandemic is under control. Discuss the results you accomplished while working remotely.

QUESTIONS TO ASK
EMPLOYERS ABOUT COVID-19

The coronavirus pandemic has created many difficult situations for employees. You need to get answers to questions about safety protocols and how you will be protected in these uncertain times. Here are some questions to ask when you appear for an interview.

- *What are the company's plans for return to a traditional office?* You should find out what are the employer's plans to return to working from a traditional office, and what precautions will be taken to create a safe work environment.
- *What financial or operational challenges did your company, or business unit, face during Covid-19?*
- *To what extent did Covid-19 result in company layoffs or furloughs, and how is your level of staffing now in comparison to before?*

WHO IS INVITED FOR INTERVIEW?

A person is invited for a job interview when the employer thinks there is a possible match with job requirements. When you apply for jobs for which you are qualified and then tailor your cover letters and resume to the needs of potential employers, you are likely to get invited for job interviews.

When you submit your resume online, it goes into an Applicant Tracking System (ATS). It is a software that evaluates how far you match the requirements of the job posting. You can get past the ATS only when the resume contains many of the keywords in the job posting. Most of the resumes that go through the ATS are eliminated because they don't match the job requirements. Resumes that meet the ATS requirements are given a review to determine whether further consideration is justified. Each resume gets a few seconds glance, and if it does not stand out as a good match with job requirements, it gets discarded. The candidates who pass this initial test are invited for a short screening interview by a representative of the Human Resources Department, or receive a phone call to establish their interest and suitability. A few candidates who make it through the screening process are invited for face-to-face interviews.

The job interview is an information gathering process, both for the employer and the candidate. While the employer tries to assess whether the candidate has the required qualifications, the candidate tries to determine whether this is the right place to work. Considering that the interview is a setting for the exchange of information, it should result in both sides speaking and listening equally. The candidate should plan to speak about 50% of the time, and provide concise and relevant answers to each question. It is desirable to keep the answers in the range of 30 seconds to two minutes. An important thing to remember is to never say anything negative about a previous boss or employer.

Your success in the interview process will depend largely on the level of your preparation and positive attitude in responding to questions. You should anticipate what questions are likely to be asked during the interview, and know how you are going to answer those questions. You should have a list of questions you want to ask the interviewer. The interview is an opportunity for you to learn about the job and the employer so that you can decide if this is the right opportunity for you.

WHAT ARE THE EMPLOYER'S EXPECTATIONS?

You should keep in mind the employer's expectations when you appear for an interview, whether it is virtual or in person. If you can meet those expectations, there is high probability that you will be successful in the interview process.

Following is a summary of what the employers expect when they interview candidates.

- **First and foremost, how you come across.** This includes your dress and grooming, your eye contact, how you express yourself, your body language, your consideration for others and your overall manners. If the initial reaction is negative, the candidate is not likely to be hired.

- **Second, the impression you create about your reliability.** It includes showing up for the interview on time. When hiring a new employee, the employer wants to add someone who will be an asset and get things done. They want you to be a part of the solution to their problems. Many of the interview questions are intended to establish reliability. If a candidate comes across as unmotivated or disorganized, it is likely that someone else will get the job.

- **The third and ultimate expectation of the employer is that you possess the skills and experiences to effectively handle the job responsibilities.** You are invited for the interview because the employer believes you have the needed skills and experiences. Now it is up to you to prove that you possess the needed skills and experience in greater measure than all other candidates. This requires preparation and a clear understanding of your own capabilities as well as the job requirements. Many candidates have the needed skills, but they are not able to communicate that in the interview process.

Many career opportunities are lost because of simple mistakes such as not being on time, bad breath, limp handshake, avoiding eye contact, not remembering the names of interviewers, poor choice of clothes, bad manners, lack of consideration for others, failure to thank, and leaving the interview without an understanding of the next step.

INTERVIEW QUESTIONS AND POSSIBLE ANSWERS

Following is a list of questions often asked during job interviews.

- **Tell me about yourself.** *Suggestion:* You should limit your answer to two minutes. In addition to providing facts, emphasize the work experience you enjoyed the most and the positive results you accomplished. Point out to your strengths and good work habits. This question is a test of your ability to select the relevant portions of your background, and present that information clearly in a short time.

- **What are your major strengths?** *Suggestion:* This is an opportunity for you to focus on your personal traits such as integrity, punctuality, persistence, enthusiasm, hard work, and the ability to get along with others. You should highlight two to three traits and describe how those traits helped you to do a superior job in your previous positions.

- **What is your major weakness?** *Suggestion:* After you state a weakness, explain what you are doing to overcome it. When you mention a weakness, also point out some positive aspects associated with it.

- **Why are you interested in this position?** *Suggestion:* Describe how your skills, experiences and background match the job requirements.

- **Why do you want to leave your present job?** *Suggestion:* Say positive things about your company and your boss (whenever that is true). Emphasize how the position for which you are interviewing, offers a better opportunity to use your experience and skills. Never say anything negative about your current or previous employer.

- **Why should we hire you?** *Suggestion:* This question is uppermost in the interviewer's mind whether it is asked directly like this, or in another way. The right way to answer this question is to point out the benefits that will result to the employer by hiring you. You should offer some proof by relating how you helped your previous employers make more money by increasing sales and revenue and through reducing costs or solving problems.

- **What are your salary requirements?** *Suggestion:* The best way to answer this question is to say that you are very interested in the position, and the salary would be negotiable. You should not name a number for the desired salary at this early stage. However, if pressed for this information, give a broad, but feasible range that can help the company determine if you fit within the salary guidelines for the company. When the salary question is asked by a recruiter from executive search firm, you should clearly state your requirements. The recruiter needs to know if your salary requirements match the client guidelines, and whether you should be referred to the hiring company.

- **How does your experience relate to this job?**
  Suggestion: This is a direct question, and an opportunity to emphasize how your experience fits the job requirements. You should pick each of the major job requirements and describe how your experience would enable you to do an excellent job.

Here is a great question some interviewers use to judge the quality of the candidate they are facing. They ask: "Tell me how you spent your day yesterday". If you have a disciplined and well organized daily routine, you will probably talk about reading the newspaper and trade magazines, checking the available positions of interest, adding names and phones to your contact list, researching the companies you have targeted for job search, preparing follow-up letters and thank you notes, making follow-up phone calls, and doing your favorite exercise routine to keep your body in shape. On the other hand, persons who are not focused and organized will probably show their true character. This is a good way for employers to rule out unsuitable candidates.

Some additional questions during job interviews include the following:

- Tell me about your performance in your most recent position.
- What are your short-term and long-term goals?
- Tell me about the most difficult boss you have ever had.
- What do you think is the next step in your career path?
- What position do you expect to have in five years?
- What is your ideal job, and Why?
- What steps have you taken to improve yourself in the last six months?
- What is your greatest accomplishment? And, disappointment?

- Who was your best teacher?
- Who was your best boss?
- How do you manage stress?
- What qualities do you look for in members of your team?
- Why did you leave your last job?
- What did you like the most about your last job?
- What was the greatest accomplishment in your last job?
- What was the major disappointment in your last job?
- Why do you think we should offer you this position?
- When do you think you can start if we offered you this position?
- Are you willing to relocate? Any geographic preferences?
- How much were you paid in your last job?
- What is the last book you read?
- How do you measure success?
- What job would you select if you had the choice to pick any job?

These are some of the frequently asked questions. You may want to develop a concise response to each question, and to practice it before the interview. Your responses should highlight your accomplishments and strengths.

There is a new trend in interview questions designed to rattle candidates who have well-rehearsed answers to frequently asked questions. This trend started with technology companies, and now interviewers in other industries too are getting on the bandwagon of asking creative questions that do not relate directly to the job requirements, or to the candidate's background. These questions are bizarre, and the primary objective is to see how the candidate would react in an unexpected situation. Here are some examples of the strikingly unconventional questions: If someone decided to write a book about you, what should be the title? If you had wings, where would you like to fly to and why? If you were asked to compare yourself with an animal, which would be the animal you pick and why? There is no right or wrong answer to these questions. The interviewer is just trying to assess how you react in an unexpected situation. There is no way of knowing what creative questions might be asked during an interview. When you appear for an interview, try to be confident and relaxed, and preparation for answering conventional questions would give you that feeling. If creative and unconventional questions do come up, listen carefully and respond promptly rather than looking perplexed. Do take enough time to formulate your answer, but not too much time. The interviewer is expecting a response, and trying to judge how you react in unexpected and difficult situations. Answering too quickly or becoming baffled is a reaction that signals a weak candidate. For more details on how to be successful in behavioral interviews, you may want to review the section on behavioral interviews included later in this chapter.

Interview Preparation

In preparing for the job interviews, you should keep one question uppermost in your mind: Why should they hire me over all the other candidates?

You need to be fully prepared for the interview. Preparation will give you a sense of confidence, which is critical during the interview. In addition, the preparation will enable you to focus on the job requirements and how your skills and experiences match those requirements. Here is good advice from Abraham Lincoln on preparing for interviews. He said: "When I am getting ready to reason with a man, I spend one-third of my time thinking about myself and what I am going to say and two-thirds about him and what he is going to say". When preparing for interviews, your primary focus should be on researching the employer, reviewing the job requirements, and anticipating the questions they are likely to ask you during the interview.

The following are some suggestions to get ready for an interview.

- **Confirm arrangements:** Get confirmation of the time, date, location, and a contact phone number. Also get the names and titles of the persons who will interview you. If you received a confirmation letter or e-mail, take it with you.

- **Learn about the job:** You should study the job description, and understand the principal responsibilities and requirements. You should have a clear picture in your mind of requirements and how your skills and experiences match those requirements. You want to highlight those parallels during the interview. If you did not get a copy of the job description, ask the person scheduling the interview, to send you the job description prior to the interview. Most employers will readily comply with your request, and they will be impressed with your interest in learning more about the opportunity. You might want to find out how long the position has been vacant, and why the person in that position left. If it is a new position, try to find out the reason it was created and what results are expected. Also, try to find out who will interview you first and what additional interviews are expected. You should try to get as much information as possible about the persons who will interview you.

- **Learn about the company:** You should research the employer organization. This is an essential step for interview preparation. You should know about the company's mission, values, history, management team, major clients, and operating results. You should find out how long the company has been around, and what is its history. What are their plans and objectives? Such information is usually available on the company's website, trade directories, and in annual report for a public company. Learn as much as you can about the organization. This will enable you to effectively respond to questions during the interview, and ask intelligent and appropriate questions. Employers expect you to know information about the company before you appear for the interview.

- **Plan appropriate clothes for the interview:** This depends on the industry and the job for which you are interviewing. A two-piece matching business suit is usually appropriate when you are interviewing for a professional position. When in doubt, ask the person who is scheduling the interview about the attire that would be appropriate for your interview.

- **Prepare documents to take to the interview:** You should take with you the confirmation letter you received for the interview, extra copies of your resume, job description for the position, and a pad in a holder for taking notes.

- **Anticipate questions and have your own list of questions to ask:** The employer's objective is to evaluate the candidate's skills, qualities, and experience level as related to the job requirements. Your objective is to convince the interviewer that you are the right candidate for the position. Your response to each question should be clear and relevant to what is being asked. You should grasp the question before starting to answer. If you do not understand the question, ask for clarification. Provide a concise answer, and ask the interviewer if further details are needed. Focus on your strongest skills and experiences as they relate to job requirements. You should always be honest during the interview. Never say something that you know is not true.

Candidate's Questions

You must decide whether this opportunity is right for you, just as the employer is trying to decide whether you are the right candidate. The interview enables you to learn about the company and the position and to determine whether you want to pursue this opportunity. You need a comprehensive list of questions to evaluate the opportunity. In preparing your list of questions, avoid asking for information that is in the literature you received from the employer or on the company website.

Questions are the best way for you to get the information you need, and at the same time, demonstrate that you understand the company and the job requirements. Asking the right questions will set you apart from other candidates. Keep your questions short and simple, but avoid asking questions that can be answered with a simple "yes" or "no". Ask open-ended questions that require the interviewer to give a detailed answer. That will create opportunities for exchange of additional information.

Some questions you may want to ask to develop your knowledge and understanding of the employer include:

- What is the company's strength as compared to competitors?
- What are the career growth opportunities in this position?

- What is the organizational structure and how does the position fit?
- How would you describe a typical work day for this position?
- How much overnight travel is needed?
- What is the biggest opportunity facing the company?
- What are the priorities for this position?
- What is the company looking for in the ideal candidate?
- What skills are needed the most to succeed in this position?
- How employees are evaluated for their contributions?
- What are the company's expectations from this position?
- What are the skills and experiences of the most successful employees?
- When does the employer expect to reach a decision?
- What is the next step in the hiring process?

Always listen carefully when your questions are being answered. You should respond and ask follow-up questions as needed.

Interview Tips

Plan to arrive at the interview location a few minutes before the scheduled time for the interview. You cannot afford to be late for the interview. If you are not going to be able to make it on time, be sure to call the interviewer's office. Turn off your cell phone before you walk into the employer's office, and let the receptionist know you are there. If possible, check yourself out in a mirror just before you go into the interview. Always treat receptionists and other employees with the utmost respect. Hiring managers often ask everyone who interacted with the candidate for their impressions.

First impression is critical. And, you get only one chance to make a good first impression.

First impression is formed in less than 30 seconds. It is based on your appearance, behavior, and body language. Appropriate professional dress, a firm handshake, a smile on your face, eye contact, and a sense of confidence as you walk into the interviewer's office will help you to make a good first impression. Look around the interviewer's office and observe what is on the desk and on the walls. You may find some areas of common interest that you can weave into your conversation during the interview.

Here are some additional tips to follow during an interview.

- **Maintain a professional approach:** Some interviewers are very casual. Do not let this drop your professionalism. Do not interrupt, always wait until the interviewer has finished. Do not smoke or chew gum during the interview.

- **Keep a note pad handy:** Write down the names and positions of the persons you are meeting. Try to get their business cards.

- **Pay attention to non-verbal behavior:** Your body language plays a key role in the interview process. You should sit straight and maintain eye contact with the interviewer. Your eye contact demonstrates your interest and confidence. When a person looks away while talking to someone, it shows lack of interest. Eye contact can make a big difference in how you are perceived by the interviewer. Always maintain eye contact with the interviewer when answering a question.

- **Appear enthusiastic and confident:** Remain enthusiastic and positive during the interview. Never make a negative comment about a previous employer or any other person. Focus on positive things such as your accomplishments. Remain enthusiastic, and at the same time, avoid appearing pushy and trying very hard to sell yourself.

- **Listen carefully:** This is an essential interview skill, and often neglected due to the desire to quickly answer questions. Listen by paying attention to every spoken word and by observing non-verbal expressions of the interviewer. Always remember, never interrupt the interviewer. Wait for the interviewer to finish answering a question before asking for any additional information.

- **Remember names:** You need to develop the ability to remember names. This is one of the most important things taught in the Dale Carnegie courses. Pick up a copy of the book "How to Win Friends and Influence People" by Dale Carnegie. The book has some valuable tips for remembering names.

- **Give concise and honest answers:** Your answers should be concise and to the point. When you do not understand a question, ask for clarification. Do not talk at great length. Most questions should be answered in less than two minutes. If you need more than two minutes to answer a question, pause for a moment, and ask the interviewer whether you should go into more detail. Any long answers should be avoided. Do not bring up subjects unrelated to the question being asked. The interview is a two-way street. You should plan to ask questions and draw out the interviewer. Those questions will help you decide if you are really interested in the job. The candidate should not speak for more than half of the time.

- **Focus on your accomplishments:** The objective during the interview should be to demonstrate how you fit the job requirements. You should focus on your accomplishments as they relate to the job responsibilities. A good interviewer would be looking for examples of your achievements, specifically how you solved a problem or initiated an improvement.

- **Come across as a team player:** While you focus on your accomplishments, you also want to come across as a team player. It is important to point out how others helped you and you helped them. Employers want to hire those who will be good team players while they get the job done.

- **Ask for the next step:** Before leaving the interview, always ask about the next step. Reiterate your interest in the position, emphasize how you are qualified to fill it, and ask if there is any additional information you need to submit in support of your candidacy. Don't be afraid to ask for a job offer on the spot. If they are not willing to make a job offer then and there, you at least want to know when you will be invited for another interview.

Be aware that gestures and other nonverbal communications strongly influence the impression you create. Failure to make eye contact will hurt your chances of getting a job. Other body language mistakes to avoid are: weak handshake, not smiling, bad posture, nervousness, and distracting hand gestures. Being prepared is the best way to avoid these mistakes. Practice in front of someone and rehearse in front of a mirror.

You must create a clear impression of what you can do for the company and why they should hire you. Your purpose is to sell yourself, and leave the interviewer with a clear understanding of how you are the best candidate for the position.

Interview Follow-up

After the interview, you should plan to take the following steps:

- **Make detailed notes of significant discussions during the interview.** This information will be helpful to you during subsequent conversations with the employer. The information you record for future use should include: names, titles, phone numbers, and addresses of the persons you met; job description and any additional information provided during the interview; whether relocation is required; career advancement opportunities within the company; what is the next step in the interviewing process; when decision is expected; why are you still interested in the position; and how your skills and experiences match what the job requires.

- **Call the recruiter at the executive search firm if you were referred by a search firm.** The recruiter would want to know your level of interest in the opportunity for further discussions with the potential employer.

- **Send a letter or an e-mail message to thank the interviewer.** This should be done as soon as possible after the interview. You should express your gratitude for the interviewer's time, and reiterate your interest in the position and your confidence in your qualifications for the job.

- **Do not burn the bridges behind you.** If another candidate is selected for the position, you may want to send a note to the recruiter from the executive search firm or the employer indicating your interest in being considered for a similar position in the future.

Second Interview

The top candidates for a position are generally invited for second interviews. These interviews usually take place on-site where the candidate will be working. The candidate will meet with several persons, including the immediate boss, one or two colleagues, someone from the Human Resources department, and sometimes the department head or a member of the senior management team. This is usually the last step before the hiring decision is made.

The employer's objective is to identify the best candidate who has the required skills, qualities, and experiences, and will fit nicely into the organization. Your goal is to see if this is the company, the job, the work environment, and the associates you want.

The following are some tips for the second interview.

- **Get detailed information:** Find out the date, time, and place of interview, and the names and titles of the interviewers. If you are coming from out of town, find out who will arrange for travel and lodging, and how will you get from where you will stay to the interview location.
- **Research the hiring company:** Collect information about the company, the job, and the people who will conduct the second interview. You may be able to get such information on the company's website or obtain it from the person who conducted the first interview.
- **Salary expectations:** You may be asked to give the minimum salary acceptable to you. One way to answer

this question is to give a salary range acceptable to you, depending on bonus and other benefits.

- **Be ready to handle in-depth questions:** The second interview usually involves more interviewers, in-depth questions, higher intensity and greater pressure. There may be more focus on behavioral questions; a section explaining behavioral interviews is provided later in this chapter.

- **Determine what the employer is looking for in this position:** You should look for the clues as the interviewers are speaking, or at some point, simply ask the question, "What are the most important skills and experiences you are seeking for this position". You can then position the responses to highlight your skills and experiences that match those requirements.

- **Ask your questions:** This is your opportunity to decide whether you want the job. Ask all the questions on your list. Observe the environment around you to determine whether you want to be a part of it. If this is the job you want, reiterate your interest as you meet with the interviewers. This is an opportunity to build a relationship with the person to whom the position reports. It is quite appropriate to ask when that person started working for the company, positions held, and the most satisfying aspects of working for the company.

When the interview ends, express thanks to each interviewer and reiterate your interest in the position. After you return, send follow-up letters to thank each interviewer and to state how your skills and experiences match the job requirements.

Interview during a Meal

Interviews during meals enable employers to observe your table manners and social conduct while you answer and ask questions.

Your interactions in a social setting are particularly important if you are interviewing for a sales position or a position that requires contact with clients or other entities.

The dining etiquette requires that you follow the lead of the interviewer. You should wait for your interviewer to sit before you sit. Let the interviewer order the meal first. It is wise to follow the interviewer's lead in ordering your meal. You may order the same thing or something close to the price of the meal the interviewer ordered. If the interviewer orders desert and coffee, it will be polite for you to do the same.

You should sit up straight during the meal, and do not cross your legs. You should avoid ordering items that require a lot of handling because that may distract you from answering questions. Stay away from meals that are messy such as spaghetti or corn on the cob. You should order a small meal and the type of food you can easily manage. Above all, avoid ordering alcohol. You should order a soft drink even if the interviewer has ordered wine or beer. And, do not smoke even if the interviewer is smoking.

You need to remember the basic table manners: place napkin on your lap, keep your hands and elbows off the table, and be polite to the staff. At the completion of the meal, fold your napkin and place it to the left side of your plate (do not put it on the plate). Do not criticize the quality of food or service.

Meal interviews are just as important as office interviews. Remember you are being judged for your social manners, in addition to your answers to interview questions. Focus more on communicating with the interviewer, and not on handling your meal. The interview is a two-way process. You should have your own questions so that you can engage the interviewer to do as much talking as you do.

Keep in mind that the main purpose of the interview, combined with a meal, is to evaluate your social interactions. Eating is secondary. You don't want to be talking with food in your mouth. Take small bites so that you can answer questions promptly. The interviewer may ask serious questions, and so be ready to provide appropriate answers just as you would in an office interview situation. At the end of the meal, thank the interviewer. Also remember to send a thank-you note the same day.

Behavioral Interviews

Behavioral interviewing is a style of interviewing which requires you to answer open-ended questions about situations you have been in and how you responded to those situations.

During a behavioral interview, you need to describe a real project or experience, how you dealt with it, and the result. Such interviewing is based on the belief that past performance is the best indicator of future behavior. Before the interview, you should focus on details of your past accomplishments and how you were able to achieve your results. The interviewer will have a lot of follow-up questions to understand your motivation and behavior pattern. Accordingly, it is important to describe a situation that highlights one or more of your transferable skills and which can be described in enough detail to demonstrate your capabilities.

Examples of behavioral questions include:
- Describe a difficult situation where you showed initiative.
- Tell me about a difficult boss and how you interacted.

- Describe a complex project, and how you completed it.
- Tell me about a risky decision you made, and why you made it.
- Describe your greatest accomplishment in your last position.
- Tell me about a disappointment and how you benefited from it.
- Describe the most stressful situation you have handled.
- Tell me about a situation you now think you should have handled differently.
- Describe how you used your presentation skills to influence others.
- Describe your leadership positions and how you contributed in those positions.

Some interviewers just ask an open-ended question: "Tell me about yourself" and use your response to ask probing questions about your experiences and background. You should make a list of your skills and qualities that match the job requirements. The closer you are to meeting the job requirements, and presenting yourself as the best candidate for the job, the greater the probability that you will be hired.

Behavioral interviewing is a technique used to predict your future behavior based on the evaluation of your past behavior. Here are some suggestions to prepare you for the behavioral interview. First, make a list of the skills required for the position. Second, make a list of your skills and experiences related to the position. Third, put together detailed descriptions of how you handled specific situations.

You must be very frank and honest in answering questions. We all make mistakes and learn from them. Do not try to hide your past mistakes. The interviewer is not looking for perfection, but for behavioral patterns and how a person has progressed. Be concise in your answers. The interviewer is looking for a brief description of the problem, what action you took and why, and what was the outcome.

Above all, be honest. A good behavioral interviewer will ask questions of increasing detail to get a complete picture of your behavior during a challenging situation. This interviewing style can highlight inconsistencies in a story. It is important to describe only those situations in which you played a major role and that you can recall in sufficient detail.

References

Because of remote interviews sparked by the pandemic, references have become more important. Sometimes employers do not meet new hires until they report to work. They consider references not just a formality, but a necessity. Also reference checks have become more thorough. They may be asked to recreate work situations to provide examples of problem solving by candidates. Employers proceed with the assumption that references will say nice things. Anything less than high praise of the candidate may trigger a red flag.

You will need three to six names for your reference list. At least one reference should be your boss in a prior position. Other references can be colleagues and clients in previous positions.

You need references who can attest to your work ethic and performance on the job. Your reference list should include the name, title, company name, e-mail address, and a phone number together with a brief description of the person's relationship to you. Take your reference list to interviews, or be ready to submit it immediately after the interview to the employer or the executive search firm.

You should establish your references at the start of the job search process. While companies usually do not contact references until just before making a job offer, some search firms like to check references before presenting candidates to client organizations. You should be very careful in selecting your references, and then properly communicate with them so that they will be able to provide accurate and comprehensive answers regarding your suitability for the position.

Here are some suggestions to help you manage your references.

- **Select references who can speak about your work performance.** This may include supervisors, peers, co-workers, and direct reports. This may also include clients and vendor representatives. You may include academic references if you recently completed your education.

- **You may include persons who have retired or moved on to new positions.** The essential requirement is that they should have direct knowledge of your work performance, personal qualities and capabilities.

- **Always obtain permission of the persons you have selected to serve as your references.** Determine when they would like to be contacted, and at what phone numbers.

- **Provide your resume to your references and let them know about the kind of position you are seeking**. Refresh their memory regarding their work experience with you including when you worked for them, for how long, in what position, and what were your strengths and most important contributions.

- **Advise your references whenever you give their names to potential employers or search firms.**
- **Whenever you accept a new position or reject an offer, be sure to contact your references and thank them for their help and support.**

References are an extremely important resource. You should cultivate them, and keep them informed about your job search progress.

While references have become less popular because of information about candidates available on LinkedIn and other social media websites, some companies will not hire a new employee without checking references.

Interview Success

The following guidelines will help you succeed in the interview process.

- **Be fully prepared:** You must be well prepared to do well during the interview. Many candidates walk into an interview without having researched the company and the position. You are going to be compared with all other candidates, and unless you prove yourself to be the best candidate, you will not get the job offer. To be the best in anything, you must be thoroughly prepared.
- **Prove that you are the best candidate:** Remember you are the seller, and interviewer is the buyer. It is up to you to prove to the interviewer that you are the best candidate. If another candidate can demonstrate better suitability for the position, you are not going to get a job offer. You are in a competition, and you must prove that you are the best suited candidate. Do not leave it just up to the interviewer to decide the best candidate. Take it upon yourself to prove that you are the

best candidate by highlighting your best skills and traits that match the job requirements. Plan your presentation and your answers to interview questions with the goal of demonstrating that you are the best candidate. Believe in yourself as the best candidate.

- **Know how you will benefit the employer:** You must know how you fit the job requirements before you walk into the interview. This means, a careful study of the job description and review of your skills and experiences as a match for those requirements is needed. Your ability to communicate that to the interviewer, as compared to how other candidates communicate such information, will determine who gets the job offer.

Companies hire the person who comes across as the best overall candidate. Candidates with excellent technical qualifications sometimes get rejected because they did not give good answers to interview questions. In addition to technical skills, companies are looking for employees with the right attitude and the ability to communicate and interact with others.

Your focus during the interview process should be on what you can offer the company, not what the company can offer you. Positive attitude is a great asset in the interview process. It will result in better interactions with the interviewer. Reflect on your accomplishments and success stories as you are going to the interview. Never say a bad thing about a former boss or employer as that could convey the impression that you are a negative person

Thank-you Notes

Consider this as an essential part of the interview process. Showing appreciation and gratitude is always good, and it is even more important during job search. Always send a thank-you note to everyone who helped you in the interview process.

You need to show your appreciation to interviewers for their time and consideration. You can do this by email if that is the way you were communicating prior to the interview. Plan to do this within 24 hours after the interview. Email notes have one clear advantage. They are a quick way to remain in contact with the company. However, it is a good idea to also follow-up with a letter by regular mail. This is an opportunity for you to distinguish yourself from other candidates. You can send a handwritten note or a typed letter. I prefer personalized typed letters that pick up on what was discussed during the interview. A thank-you note should accomplish the following:

- Show your appreciation for the interviewer's time.
- Reiterate how your skills and background match the job requirements.
- Show your enthusiasm for the job.

A thank-you note is a good way to demonstrate your interest in the job and how you match the job requirements. It is a good way to refresh the interviewer's memory of meeting with you.

CHAPTER 7

NEGOTIATING SALARY AND BENEFITS

The most difficult thing in any negotiation, almost, is making sure that you strip it of the emotion and deal with the facts.
—Howard Baker

A job offer is subject to negotiation. You can negotiate the base salary, bonus, relocation package, benefits, stock compensation, severance terms, and anything else in the job offer.

It feels wonderful to get a job offer. This is what you were striving for when you started your job search. But do not rush to say "yes".

The roles are suddenly reversed when you get a job offer. Now you have become the buyer. The employer is now trying to sell you on the career opportunity, salary, and benefits. They want you, and in most cases, would like you to join as soon as possible. You must decide whether you want them, and if so, what changes are needed in the job offer before you make a commitment.

Is this the right job?

Here are some questions you should try to answer to determine if this is the right job.
- Are you sure this job is a good match with your skills?
- Will this job put you on the career path you want?

- Do you feel you will have a good working relationship with your boss?
- What is this company's reputation in the industry?
- Do you have a clear understanding of the job description?
- Are you convinced that you will succeed in this job?
- How does your family feel about this job?
- Will you enjoy working with people you met during the interview process?

You need to make a decision that will have a long-range impact on your career path. Fortunately, most companies give you a few days to make your decision. You have probably determined, before a job offer is presented to you, that the company is a good place to work and you are satisfied with the position and advancement opportunities. If you have any concerns about the company or the position, this is the time to take another look at what you may be getting into. No amount of salary or benefits will make up for a bad career choice. Assuming you are satisfied with the company and the position, take a close look at the financial aspects.

Job offers are subject to negotiation. You can negotiate the job responsibilities, base salary, bonuses, relocation package, benefits, stock compensation, severance terms and anything else included in the job offer. This is an opportunity for you to define what you want and what you can get, and then negotiate an employment package acceptable to you.

Timing is a critical factor in negotiating. The ideal time to negotiate is when you have received a verbal offer from the employer, or through an executive search firm. Prepare a logical explanation for every change you want to request. Remember, negotiating is a two-way process, where both you and the employer try to reach an agreement that will be beneficial to both sides.

Preparation is the key to good negotiations

You need to research, consider alternatives, plan and effectively communicate with the employer. You need to know how far you can go, and when to pull back. When the job being offered to you is hard to fill, the employer will be more accommodating. If other candidates are available to fill the position, the employer may be less inclined to negotiate the terms of the job offer. Smaller companies are more willing to negotiate as compared to larger organizations with standard policies and procedures.

There is a big difference in salaries for the same jobs in different parts of the country. You should look up cost of living data when researching salaries. Here are some websites for your research.

www.jobstar.org

This is a wonderful resource for help on salary information. It helps you connect to over 300 free online salary surveys. The surveys come from several kinds of sources including: General periodicals; local newspapers; Trade and professional journals; Trade and professional associations; and Recruiters or employment agencies. This website also offers helpful links to advice on salary negotiation strategies.

www.salary.com

This is a leading provider of on-demand human resources software to help businesses and individuals manage pay and performance, and achieve greater results in the workplace. The website includes quick links to compensation-related information: Salary Wizard; Benefits Calculator; Executive Pay

Wizard; Cost of Living Calculator; Premium Salary Report; Salary Wizard Canada; Performance Self-Test; and Salary Negotiation Advice.

www.salaryexpert.com

This website was launched in 2000 to provide reports on salaries and cost of living. Tools available on this website help people make informed decisions when planning careers and searching for jobs. Following career tools are available: Search Jobs by Salary; Cost of Living Calculator; Education Planning Center; Job Search; Career Salary Potential Report; and Student Cost of Living Report.

www.payscale.com

Payscale is a market leader in global online compensation data. It has one of the largest databases of online employee salary data in the world. This website offers salary reports based on your job title, location, education, skills and experience.

www.bls.gov

This is an official website of the United States government. It is managed by the U.S. Bureau of Labor Statistics. It covers information on a wide range of subjects related to employment and labor. For Pay and Benefits, it provides information on employment costs, national compensation data, wage data by area and occupation, earnings by demographics, earnings by industry, county wages, benefits, and compensation research. It is a nationally recognized source of career information.

JOB OFFER GUIDELINES

The following guidelines should help you in job offer negotiations.

- **Do not immediately accept what you are offered:** Always ask for some time to consider an offer. Most employers are willing to give you a couple of days to consider and respond to a job offer. It is a mistake to jump at an offer, and accept it right away. Talk to your family members and some professionals to determine whether it is a fair offer before you accept it. Accepting something less than what you are worth will not only give you less income now, but also set you back in terms of future income as raises are a percentage of what you are earning.

- **Do not reject the offer quickly:** Some candidates make the mistake of rejecting an offer too quickly because the salary offered is below their expectations. Always look at the total package rather than just the salary component. Some companies offer larger bonuses, stock options, and benefits. You may still find that the total package does not meet your expectations, but do take time to review it carefully and see if you can negotiate some aspects of it to make it acceptable.

- **Do not tell the employer what you will accept:** It is a mistake for a candidate to bring up the subject of salary during job interviews. You should leave it to the employer to initiate this discussion. Employers may ask for your salary history, and you should give accurate information. They may also ask for your salary expectation, and you should give that in a broad range pointing out that it would depend upon the total package such as bonus and benefits.

- **Do not tell the employer what you need for living expenses:** You will get what you are worth in the eyes of the employer and nothing more. You must focus on the value you bring to the employer. Never tell an employer the amount of money you need for the living expenses. That has no relevance to the employer.

- **Know your market value:** Many candidates start thinking about their market value only after getting a job offer. You should do that before you interview for jobs. There are many resources available on the Internet such as www.salary.com and www.salaryexpert.com. Also, you should talk to some professionals in the employment industry. They can usually tell the salary range you can expect based on your education and experience level.

- **Focus on one or two changes in the offer:** While employers may be willing to make one or two changes in the offer, most of them will not negotiate the entire package. You should focus on one or two elements that are most critical to you. If the salary is too low, ask for a change. If the employer will not change the salary, try to get more in terms of bonus, stock options or benefits.

- **Never burn your bridges behind you:** Negotiating a job offer is the beginning of the working relationship with an employer, and it is essential to conduct negotiations in a professional and respectful manner even if you and the employer do not see eye to eye. If you decide to decline an offer, do so in a professional way so that there may be a future opportunity for you to connect with this employer.

- **Always get the job offer in writing:** Any good employer would be willing to state the offer in writing. If an employer is not willing to do so, re-consider whether you want to work in that place. Whatever special arrangements you can negotiate should be documented in writing. If you get a special bonus arrangement, additional vacation time, earlier salary review, get it all in writing. It is possible that the person who negotiated special arrangements with you could move on to another assignment. You want to make sure that you will get whatever was agreed. Sometimes you may just have to spell out the special arrangements in a letter to the hiring manager, get the manager to acknowledge it and put it in your personnel file.

- **Evaluate the benefits package:** Employers offer a wide variety of benefits to attract and retain employees. You should consider the benefits package before accepting or declining a job offer. The benefits offered by employers may include medical insurance, dental insurance, eye care insurance, life insurance, accidental death insurance, disability insurance, business travel insurance, vacation, holidays, sick/personal days, retirement plans, profit sharing, stock options, tuition reimbursement, membership in health clubs, on-site child care facilities, parking reimbursement, transportation to and from work, company car, and mobile phone.

- **Understand the entire offer:** Make sure you understand all aspects of the job offer, including salary, bonus, stock option plan, non-competition agreement, performance review plan, paid time off policy, and benefits package. If you don't understand any aspect of the job offer, don't hesitate to ask the employer. Your first day on the job is not the time to find out about your compensation package and the company policies.

- **Review all employment documents:** Ask for copies of all documents you will be required to sign upon accepting the position. This will often include an employment letter, a non-disclosure agreement, and may include a non-compete agreement. Review these documents carefully and seek the assistance of an attorney if there are terms of employment you do not understand. These agreements will not only govern during your employment, but may define certain obligations after you terminate employment.

JOB OFFER CHECK LIST

Following items are generally included in a job offer.

- **Job title:** This is an important consideration when you are changing jobs. You may not want to accept a lower job title than your current position. Companies have some flexibility in this area, and you want to pay attention to it when you receive a verbal job offer. Some companies state that job title is not an important part of their corporate culture, but remember that the next company you work for may not feel the same way. Be sure to negotiate a job title that is suitable for your skills and qualifications and fits your long-term career goals.

- **Contract term:** Most jobs are offered on an employment-at-will basis, which can be terminated by either the employee or employer with a notice of two weeks. However, senior managers are sometimes provided with contracts of one year or more in duration that guarantee employment during the term of the contract. If your offer includes an employment contract, make sure you understand all the terms and conditions of that contract. In many cases, employment contracts will include non-compete agreements which are described in more detail below.

- **Non-compete agreements:** Some companies require employees, particularly in sales positions, to sign non-compete agreements to prevent them from going to work for competitors or disclose trade secrets. You want to make sure that the non-compete agreement you are signing is not so broad that you will not be able to accept a job in the same industry or geographical area. If there is a non-compete clause in your agreement, review it very carefully to make certain that you are not limiting your future opportunities. Some employers are willing to negotiate the terms of non-compete agreements.

- **Reporting relationships:** This defines your position and role in the employer organization. You want to be sure who will you report to, and the positions you will supervise. Sometimes you may not have had the opportunity to meet with the person you will report to. In such situations, you should consider asking to meet that person before accepting the job offer.

- **Start date:** You need to give the required notice to your current employer. It is generally two weeks, but may be different in your situation. You should try to leave your current employer on a happy note. If your help is required to complete any pending projects, you should try to accommodate your current employer. If you feel comfortable doing so, it is advisable to confer with your current employer before providing a firm start date to your new employer.

- **Salary:** You should find out how you will be paid (weekly, bi-weekly, or monthly) and whether you will receive a check or direct deposit to your bank account.

- **Salary review schedule:** Establish when you will get your first salary review. If you have negotiated a salary review that is outside the company's standard policies, make sure that the salary review date is indicated in your job offer letter. It is also a good idea to discuss the criteria used by the company to determine performance-based salary increases and bonuses. For small companies that may not have established employee review policies, it is strongly recommended to negotiate salary reviews as part of the job offer.

- **Bonus plan:** Determine whether you are eligible for bonus, and if so, how the bonus amounts will be calculated and the frequency of payment. Again, if the bonus plan you negotiated is different from the standard company policy, make sure it is indicated in your job offer letter.

- **Commissions:** This is particularly important for sales positions. You need to know how the commissions will be calculated and when payments will be made. If your compensation has a heavy commission component, make sure that you understand the details of the commission plan, and how sales quotas are assigned. In some cases, employers would be willing to share information about the prior year's commission payments. Review this information to make sure it meets your expectations of commission earnings.

- **Signing bonus:** Establish the amount of signing bonus, if any, and when it will be paid. In most cases, employers will require the signing bonus to be returned if the employee leaves or is terminated within a short time frame of being hired. Do not try to negotiate this point as it shows lack of commitment to the opportunity.

- **Relocation assistance:** If the employer has a relocation policy, get a copy, and establish that you will be covered under it. When there is no relocation policy, determine a flat amount to cover relocation, or get the employer's agreement to cover relocation expenses such as moving of household goods, temporary housing at new location, and other moving expenses such as termination of current lease.

- **Stock options and restricted stock units:** Establish whether you will be eligible for stock options or restricted stock units and how the granting will be determined. Make sure you understand how the stock exercise price is determined, vesting schedule, and for how long you can exercise options after they have vested. There is a significant amount of information available for public companies such as stock price history, number of shares outstanding, and market cap. You should review this information so that you can properly estimate the value of the equity component in the overall compensation package.

- **Medical coverage**: Determine what type of coverage you will have for yourself and your family members and whether dental expenses will be covered.

- **Cost of benefits:** What costs such as medical coverage you will be required to pay to cover yourself and your family members.

- **Vacation policy:** Determine the company's policy on vacations. The company may have some flexibility, especially if you are getting more vacation time in your current position.

- **Company car:** Determine whether you will be getting a company car and what type of vehicle. If company car is not included in your package, determine how you will be reimbursed for business use of personal vehicle.

- **Transportation to and from work:** Determine whether the company will provide transportation service to and from work or whether the company will cover transportation costs.

- **Parking expenses:** Determine whether the company will provide a parking space or reimbursement for parking expenses.
- **At home stipend:** Determine whether the company will provide a stipend for at-home work expenses such as Wi-Fi and equipment to make working from home easier.
- **Severance pay:** This is the time to establish what type of severance pay you will get if your services are terminated for any reason, other than cause. Severance arrangements, like employment contracts, are usually reserved for senior management.
- **Standard benefits package:** This may include life insurance, disability insurance, holidays, sick days, tuition reimbursement, health club membership, on-site child care facilities, business expense reimbursement, lap-top, and mobile phone. While you want to be aware of what is available in the standard benefits package, it is unlikely that the company would be willing to consider any changes in it except for senior level management positions.

A technique I have found very useful in evaluating my alternatives is to write down the positive and negative aspects of making a choice. I take a sheet of paper and make two columns. On one side, I put down the positive aspects of making that choice, and on the other side I write the negative aspects. After I have spent a day or two thinking about the reasons for and against making a choice, and put those reasons on a sheet of paper, the answers often becomes obvious. You may want to use something like this to evaluate the job offer you have received and how it compares to your current position or another job offer you may be considering.

You should look for possible ways to upgrade your job offer. But sometimes it can backfire. A job offer can be lost if the employer thinks you are being unreasonable. You should negotiate in a congenial manner leaving some wiggle room for yourself. Most employers expect candidates to negotiate. But they expect candidates to focus on the total job offer rather than just the salary. You can ask for a signing bonus or an early appraisal. Asking for an early appraisal shows you are willing to prove your value. Employer may agree to give you an appraisal and a raise in a shorter time. Whatever you decide to negotiate, it is important to do it in a very tactful way.

Money is not the most important thing in a new job. The financial package should be reviewed in terms of other considerations such as job responsibilities and growth opportunities. Look at the total package and how the job fits into your career goals.

CHAPTER 8

HOW TO BUILD
A HAPPY CAREER

Choose a job you love, and you will never have to work a day in your life.
—Confucius

Career development is an ongoing process that continues throughout one's working life.

A career consists of a variety of jobs, each leading to a position of higher responsibility. Finding your dream job is the beginning of your journey towards a successful and rewarding career. You can start building a successful career by achieving outstanding performance on the job and demonstrating your ability to do more than the assigned job responsibilities. When you show your interest and capability to do more than what is expected of you, there is a high probability that you will get assignments of increasingly higher complexity. That leads to promotions, and financial rewards follow.

Career development affects everyone regardless of their age or position. Few people these days remain in one job or one career throughout their lives. Everyone can benefit by being proactive in managing their careers. The job world is rapidly changing. You need to be aware of the changes taking place around you, in your company, industry, and economy, and manage your career by developing goals and action plans to make your dreams come true.

We must continue to explore all career choices available to us. We should engage in an ongoing self-assessment to learn about ourselves, explore new career opportunities, develop new skills and strategies that produce results, and continue to acquire new knowledge and skills through education and training.

CAREER PLANNING

Each person has many career options available with a variety of risks and rewards associated with each option. It takes time and effort to develop the right approach. Career planning helps you to travel the path you want to take to reach your career goals. It is an essential step in the career development process.

Those with a career plan know the path they want to travel, where they want to be in the short-term and long-term, and how they are going to get there. They know what skills they need to develop further and the training and educational programs they need to pursue. They carefully consider the career options for which they are well suited, choose the options most appealing to them, and then acquire the knowledge and skills needed to pursue their goals. Since they are following the path they have set for themselves, they are likely to be highly motivated and satisfied in their jobs.

Career planning enables you to put your major strengths to good use. You must think of and put together a description of what you are good at, your accomplishments, and the compliments you have received. As you put this information in writing, you will find a career pattern emerging. You may find that you are good at dealing with people, leading teams, solving problems, handling projects or you may find other skills and qualities in you that point to career options. Now list the dreams that you want to turn into reality. These are things that inspire you, and you want to get in your life.

Think of where you are and where you want to reach. That is the bridge you want to build.

The accomplishment of career goals is possible for everyone when they know what they want, and are willing to make the required effort. While a strong desire is essential to accomplish goals, it is equally important to determine the destination one wants to reach. You can walk up to the captain of any ship standing in the harbor, and ask about the ship's destination or next port of call. The captain will know, and will also have written plans to get there. On the other hand, when you ask 100 persons in any country about their career plans, not more than ten would know their destination in the next five or ten years.

One reason people do not set career plans is because of fear of failure. True, there is a possibility that one may not accomplish the established objective. But there is even greater danger in not setting career plans. Then you do not have a destination to reach. If you study the lives of successful people, you will always find failures in their lives. They were successful because they did not give up. They kept trying, and they achieved success ultimately.

Your career choices should be based on your skills, traits, and interests. Many people pick careers just based on the glamorous rewards those careers offer. That is a mistake. One should pick a career well-suited to one's qualifications and interests, and the rewards will follow. You must love what you do to achieve growth, rewards, and a sense of personal satisfaction.

NEW JOB GUIDELINES

Starting a new job can be quite overwhelming. You are often walking into a situation where functions of existing members of a team are already well established, and some may perceive you as a threat to their job security. You must quickly establish your credentials as a team player or as a team builder when you have been hired from outside to lead an existing department.

Some companies have onboarding programs. These programs go beyond the traditional orientation programs. The objective of such programs is to make new employees productive and satisfied with their new environment. They are introduced to the company's culture, team members, job responsibilities, and performance expectations. This process helps the new employees become productive team players and perform well.

Extensive research should be the starting point in a new job. You need to read your new employer's annual report, familiarize yourself with product brochures, go to the company website to become familiar with the organization, its history, product lines, customer base, and members of the management team. In addition, you need to learn about the industry you are entering and the economic environment in which it operates. Most of the needed research should be done before your first day on the job.

When you receive your new employee orientation package, you should ask yourself: What more do I need to know to become an exceptional employee? This may point to the need to meet with some of the department managers not included in the prepared orientation program, spend time in the customer service department, or add other items to your orientation program to get ready for exceptional performance in your new job.

Those who approach their careers in a planned and systematic way will be able to accomplish what they desire. Career development is not a one-time process. You need to follow it throughout your working life. The job-for-life covenant between employer and employee no longer exists. It has been replaced by job insecurity. Career development is now a necessary skill for survival in this uncertain job market.

New Job Action Plan

You need to ask yourself the question: How do I accomplish and exceed the performance targets established for me? You must be highly proactive and engaged to be successful in your new job. You will need to develop a step-by-step plan with detailed action steps and completion dates and then implement your plan.

Here are some questions to think about, and prepare your answers in writing, when you start in a new job:

1. **What steps I need to take to be successful in my job?** You may need to talk to your boss and the person who had your job previously as well as other resource persons to develop your action plan and the sequence in which you should follow it.

2. **What are my target dates for taking each step?** It is essential to have a target date for starting and completing each step in your action plan. You need to establish a timeline to measure your progress.

3. **What are the problems I am likely to face, and how I am going to overcome those roadblocks?** It is very important to anticipate the obstacles you are likely to face, and prepare yourself for overcoming those problems. Your conversations with your boss and your colleagues would help you prepare for any problems you are likely to face.

4. **What training programs I need for personal development?** You may need to talk to a human re-

sources specialist to prepare a development program to upgrade your skills. While some training and development programs are expensive, they can yield substantial returns for both the employer and the employee.

There are many websites available with learning resources:

Coursera: This is an online course provider founded in 2012 by two Stanford University computer science professors. Coursera works with universities and other organizations to offer online courses, certificates, and degrees in a variety of subjects. You can get on-demand video lectures in subjects like business, computer science, data science, and more. You can choose from many options including free courses. You can learn more by going to the website www.coursera.org.

LinkedIn Learning: You can get the training you need with expert-led courses. They have a library of 16,000 courses and video tutorials in business skills, technology, and creative subjects. Their courses are powered by data from over 675 million LinkedIn members. You can access their website by going to www.linkedin.com.

Udemy Inc.: They are an online course provider for students and professionals. Founded in 2010, they offer courses in leadership skills, accounting and financial statement analysis, and web development. You can shop over 100,000 online courses. This is a leading global marketplace for learning and instruction. You can access their website by going to www.udemy.com.

edX: This is an online course provider created by founding partners Harvard and MIT. They provide access to 2,000 free online courses from 140 leading institutions worldwide. You can browse free online courses in a variety of subjects by going to www.edx.org.

Corporate Class Inc.: Launched in 1984, they provide executive presence and leadership training for professionals across every organizational level. Their customized training programs and approach have made them an industry leader. You may want to visit the website www.corporateclassinc.com.

Many people approach their new jobs without a plan and action steps to succeed, and therefore, they are not able to progress in their new positions. If you are willing to develop and follow an action plan for your success in the new job, you are likely to achieve exceptional results.

STRATEGIES FOR EFFECTIVENESS

Here are three strategies that have worked well for me in my business career. These are ways I used for improving my effectiveness. I highly recommend these strategies to achieve superior results.

Prioritize tasks: At the end of each business day, make a list of the five (5) most important things you must accomplish the following day. Now rank these items in terms of their importance to you. When you arrive for work the following day, handle each listed item in the order of its importance. Begin with item number one on your list, and then go on to complete the remaining items on your list in the order of their priority. Make a new list of tasks for the following day, in the order of their priority, at the end of each day. You need to make it a habit to prepare this list before going home each day. It is very easy to validate the effectiveness of this approach. Just pursue this approach for two days, and I believe you will be amazed by how much more you are able to accomplish by following the list of prioritized tasks.

Be fully prepared for every business meeting: This means preparing an agenda for what you want to accomplish in each meeting and putting together the resources to support your objective. Whenever you are in a meeting of any kind, a staff meeting or meeting with outside vendors, clients, or prospects, others in that meeting room are trying to judge you. They judge you by the way you present your thoughts and how you interact with others. The kind of impression you create at the meeting depends on how well prepared you are, how attentively you listen to others, and whether you can build rapport with others attending the meeting. Whenever I went for a meeting with a client or prospect to develop additional business, I always prepared a written statement of my objectives and how I was going to accomplish those objectives. I made it a practice to have enough copies of a prepared agenda with me and a written presentation to leave behind. When you approach a task well prepared, it is probable that you will be able to accomplish your objective.

Identify personal development needs: While most companies have training programs for their employees, and some use outside training courses and seminars, the ultimate responsibility for personal development rests with each individual employee. We live in an environment of on-going change. There are changes taking place all the time at our employers, in our industries, and in the overall economy. We need to regularly ask ourselves the question: "How can I grow my career considering the changes taking place around me?" Your answer will help you identify your personal development needs, and open new directions and opportunities for your career. You should take full advantage of training courses made available by your company, and seek out seminars and professional meetings that will help you grow your knowledge. You will be able to advance your career rapidly when you follow this strategy.

GOAL ACCOMPLISHMENT

Our mechanism is built to accomplish goals. Just like houses are built to live in, planes are built to fly, ships are built to sail, human beings are built to accomplish goals and objectives.

Here is a formula that I have used for establishing goals.

First, you must very clearly identify what you want. Your goal must be specific, and you must establish a time limit for accomplishing it. If your goal is to make money, it is not enough to say: "I want to make a lot of money". You must determine the amount of money you want to make, and establish a time limit for making that amount of money. If your goal is to lose weight, you need to decide how much weight you are going to lose, and establish a deadline for reaching your desired weight. The same principle applies to any other goal you may wish to accomplish.

Second, the goal must be written down. Until you write down your goal, it does not take on an independent identity which is essential for accomplishing it. You should look at your written down goal every day so that it makes a deep impression on your subconscious. I know from personal experience that subconscious mind will seek out ways to accomplish your goal. I am often amazed at answers that pop out from nowhere when I am trying to solve a problem.

Third, the goal must be your very own. It must be your own goal with your full commitment behind it. It must spring from within. You cannot accomplish someone else's goal. You will not stop smoking, lose weight, or accomplish anything else simply because someone else wants you to do it. It must be your very own goal.

Fourth, you must firmly believe that you will accomplish your goal. There was never a winner in a competition who did not expect to win. You must see yourself reaching the goal before you get there. You must be able to see your destination in your own mind before you arrive there. No doubt, you will have difficulties on the way to your destination. But if you keep your sight on your destination, you will arrive there. You must have a firm belief and a determination to reach your goal.

Fifth, your goal must be big and sensible at the same time. The goal must be big enough to represent a challenge that will call upon your inner resources. At the same time, it must be realistic. It is better to set progressively higher goals. I advise salespersons to do two things in setting their goals: Try to exceed their own best performance record, and at the same time, beat the person just ahead. There is no point in taking on the champion right at the start if you are an average producer. If you follow the goal setting principle of beating your own best performance record, as well as beating the person just ahead, it will not be very long before you are the person running ahead of the pack.

Sixth, put down on paper the benefits you will get by reaching that goal. You must state exactly what benefits will accrue to you when the goal is accomplished. It is very important to keep your eyes focused on why you want to accomplish the stated objective. "What is in it for me" is an essential part of the goal setting and accomplishment process. You should ask yourself whether reaching the goal will make you happier, healthier, more prosperous, more secure, more popular or bring you another benefit.

Seventh, you must develop a detailed plan of action. This should be a step-by-step guide defining how you are going to accomplish your goal. You must define what specific actions you must take starting on the first day and until you reach your goal. You should set down what knowledge and skills you need to acquire to meet your objective, and prepare the names of groups, associations, and individuals you need to work with to achieve your goal. The plan should identify the obstacles you are going to face, and how you will overcome those obstacles.

This is the planning part. Now you need to work to accomplish your goal. Goals are very much like a building. It is built step-by-step with each brick placed according to a plan. You will have a beautiful structure when you follow a plan. On the other hand, if you pile up bricks haphazardly, without a plan, the building will never be completed. Goals are the same way. You must work according to your plan, and follow that plan every day.

CAREER DEVELOPMENT PROCESS

The starting point in any career development effort is the definition of career objectives. You must state very clearly what you want. The statement of career objectives is an exploration. It is not a one-time effort. It takes place at different times in one's career. When it is done right, it puts a sense of mission in one's work life. It is a way to discover one's unique strengths and capabilities, and find the right occupation.

The process of defining what you want is a powerful first step. Once you have established your goals, you need to commit them in writing. Once you write these goals, you will unleash the power of the sub-conscious mind which will help you to accomplish your dreams. One effective approach is to write on a single page a summary of what you hope to achieve, contribute, and become in your work life.

There are basically two types of people. There are success-conscious people and there are failure-conscious people. What happens in the case of success-conscious people is that every time they succeed, it reinforces their belief that they are successful and any failure they encounter does not discourage them. You can really change your world by changing yourself from a failure-conscious to a success-conscious person.

You must think of yourself as a successful human being with a record of accomplishments who will reach greater heights of achievement in the future. Reflect upon your past and identify those events which brought you success. Try to re-create those events in your mind, think about the successful events often, and convince yourself that you are a successful person. Learn from your failures, but do not let the past failures hold you back. Concentrate on your past successes, and make a commitment to duplicate those successes in your career development. Take a sheet of paper and list your accomplishments. Make a list of what you have achieved, and what are your good qualities. You will be amazed at the things you have accomplished, and that will help you to look at yourself as a success conscious individual.

Another way to build a positive self-image is to realize that you have great potential. There are lots of high-powered computers around, but there has never been a single computer developed anywhere in the world that is more capable than the human mind. And, each one of us is blessed with a human mind. We not only have great potential, but we use only a small fraction of it. Most estimates say that we use less than 10% of our potential. Each of us has a lot of unused potential and ability.

Every individual is unique. Those who can identify what they are good at and then pursue the areas of their strength are more successful than others.

One reason why people find themselves in jobs that do not match their liking is that they are always trying to climb the ladder, from Manager to Director to Vice President and then

President. This sometimes leads people farther and farther away from what they like to do.

I remember, early in my career at American Express, I hired a sales representative who had worked for several years in pharmaceutical sales. He was a terrific sales person and able to quickly build solid relations with his clients. His sales performance was excellent, and he did a good job of training the younger sales people. I saw management potential in him and promoted him to the District Manager position, supervising a group of sales representatives. He was in that job for about four months when he walked into my office, and said that he wanted to leave American Express. I asked him why. He said he was going back to his old job. He did not like the responsibility of managing other people. I saw him a few times after he left American Express. He was happy being back with his old company, in his old job. Here is a person who knew exactly what he wanted. He did what he was good at and passionate about, and did not hesitate to walk away from a management position that did not suit his needs and desires.

Successful people are those who are doing what they enjoy. They do not necessarily have the highest academic credentials nor do they make the most money. They are not always in the top management positions.

MY EXPERIMENT WITH CAREER DEVELOPMENT

After 33 years of a successful business career, I personally went through a full-scale examination of my career and my life, and what I wanted to accomplish during the remaining years of my career.

That led to my search for a new career that has had a life changing impact on me. It was a very rewarding decision. As a result, I enjoyed a wonderful new career for ten years as a small business owner and an executive recruiter that made excellent use of my skills, traits, and interests. Let me explain this in some detail.

In 1996, I felt the need to change the direction of my work life. I was 58 years old at that time. I was working as a Senior Vice President of International Marketing at Outsourcing Solutions Inc. My job involved interacting with executives of companies in the United States as well as in several other countries. I liked my job and had a good compensation package. But I wanted something more out of my work and my life. I felt that it was time for change and a time to accomplish a new vision for myself.

I started reading books and listening to cassette tapes on building personal mission. I spent many hours making an inventory of my strengths and what I enjoyed doing.

I reached a conclusion after many hours of deliberation. I wanted to start an executive search firm in the financial services industry. But I had two problems. I had no experience in the executive search business, and no knowledge of how a small business operates.

I contacted my network of friends and business associates. While most of them encouraged me, one of my good friends thought that I was crazy to think of starting a business in a new field. He asked: "Why do you want to leave a good job"? He added: "large companies that use outside recruiters probably have their relationships well established, and even if someone gave you a search assignment, how are you going to find the right candidate and get that candidate to leave the current employer". Those were good questions, and made me think about the various aspects of the executive search business and potential obstacles I was likely to face.

I realized that the only way to get a good understanding of the executive search business was to talk to some of the people in that business.
I researched the directory of executive recruiters specializing in financial services in New York, New Jersey, and Connecticut. I prepared a target list of persons I wanted to contact including names, addresses, and telephone numbers. I put together a one-page letter and sent it to the top executives of about 150 executive search firms in the New York area. My letter gave a summary of my business background, indicated my desire to get into the executive search business, and asked whether they would be willing to meet with me. Out of the 150 top executives in the executive search business to whom I wrote, 14 of them agreed to see me. During my interviews with them, some mentioned that no one had approached them previously the way I did. Some of them tried to interest me in joining their executive search business. Most of them very generously shared information regarding their internal operations and were delighted to offer me help and assistance to get started. I was amazed by their warmth and willingness to help. I realized that one should never hesitate to ask for help, even from unknown sources. It is human nature to be kind and helpful when approached the right way.

One interview was particularly revealing. I was meeting with the Managing Director of a large executive search firm in New York City. He said: "You will not make it in the search business". I asked him why. He said I had no experience, and I should ask myself, "What do I bring to the party?" I asked that question of myself for several days. I put together a detailed list of my skills and experiences that matched the requirements for setting up and operating an executive search business. I thought very seriously about the pros and cons of what I was contemplating to get into. I reached the conclusion that I will be able to make it in the search business.

The interviews with executives in the search business were enlightening for me. They gave me insights into the operational, marketing and financial aspects of the executive search business. This prepared the foundation for me to prepare my business plan, start an executive search firm, and enjoy the most rewarding career of my life.

I was convinced that I was ready to start an executive search firm. I prepared a detailed business plan in June 1997 based on information gathered through interviews with recruiters and research of published materials.

I went to my boss, and announced my intention to resign and start an executive search firm. He was very surprised, but agreed that I could leave my position at Outsourcing Solutions Inc. in three months. This allowed sufficient time for me to transition my responsibilities to others in the company. At the same time, it gave me additional time to prepare for my business venture. **I started Mehta Consulting as an executive search firm in October 1997. My former employer, Outsourcing Solutions Inc., became my first client. I was touched when they sent me a check for $5,000 as a retainer for their first search assignment. American Express, another former employer, also became a client for my executive search business. I searched and attracted excellent management talent for both of my former employers.**

The ten years I spent in the executive search business have been the most productive years of my career.

I enjoyed what I did, and I felt good about my career. All this came about because of a diligent search for new career. I think it is always worthwhile to devote the time and attention needed for defining one's dream job.

CONCLUSION

Career development requires investment of time, effort, focus, and resources. Those who are willing to make that investment will reap rewards in terms of professional success, job satisfaction, and financial rewards.

Life is a journey. After our birth, we follow similar life cycles. We go to school, find jobs, raise families, retire and ultimately pass away. The type of life each one of us leads is different. Some are happier and more successful.

The quality of our journey through life depends upon the preparation we make for our careers. That preparation is especially important in our younger years. The preparations we make as students and in our first couple of jobs will determine the kind of careers we are able to develop. Job security no longer exists. The important thing these days is to improve your employability by developing the right skills and learning to sell yourself as a candidate.

Self-improvement is an area in which you should invest heavily. You should upgrade your skills on an ongoing basis. Attend training courses. Continue to acquire new knowledge. Improve upon what you already know. Those who are willing to accept this responsibility, and undertake the needed career development activities, will find their careers grow and prosper.

We get in life what we desire and what we prepare for.

When we aim for high accomplishments and rewards, we usually get them. I hope this book will help you to identify your skills and interests and to acquire knowledge about the job search and career development process. I have shared with you the knowledge and experiences I have gained in my life that may help you to become more successful in your career.

Job searching is one of the most important things we do in our lives. And, it is being done more frequently because of changing dynamics in the work place. When I was growing up, it was said that you should find a good employer right out of college, and hang on to your job with all ten fingers. It is very rare these days to find an employee who works for the same employer for the entire business career.

Lifetime employment with one employer is a thing of the past. Persons starting their careers now are going to move through more jobs in ten years than my generation did in their life time. This is a going to happen for two reasons. On the one hand, companies will continue to remain focused on cost management and make staff reductions as needed. On the other hand, individuals are going to feel less loyal to companies and will readily take advantage of new employment opportunities as they become available. The rapid change has certainly raised the level of insecurity in the workforce. Both employers and employees are less committed to longer term relationships. There is lack of job security, and people change jobs freely for better opportunities. This makes for a complex environment for career development.

The responsibility for your career development rests squarely on your own shoulders. If you are not ready for the next promotional step, the company will readily hire someone from the outside to fill the position. The approach these days is to let the cream rise to the top. If a company is not able to find a suitable manager from within the organization to fill an open position, there is no hesitation to hire an executive search firm to attract the needed manager from outside. Many companies paid me executive search fees of $25,000 and more for each manager I placed.

Success is not limited to any one group of people. Successful people come in all shapes and colors, and from all walks of life. Some are tall and some are short, some are born rich, some are born poor, some have a lot of education, some have no education, some are born with good health, some are born with handicaps and accomplish so much that they become inspiration for the rest of the world.

Someone has said so appropriately: Great people are ordinary people who have an extra-ordinary amount of determination.

Faith in one's ability to accomplish an objective is an essential ingredient for success. You must expect to win. To succeed in anything, you must believe that you will be successful. **Life is a self-fulfilling prophecy. You get what you expect.** When you expect good things in life that is what you will get.

Let me share with you the words of Andrew Carnegie: "Think of yourself on the threshold of unparalleled success. A whole, clear, glorious life lies before you. Achieve! Achieve!"

OVERCOMING THE ROADBLOCKS

Most of the important things in the world have been accomplished by people who have kept on trying when there seemed to be no hope at all.
—Dale Carnegie

I acquired a great lesson out of a stunning setback when I was just 14 years old attending school in Delhi, India. I was among a few students who failed in the annual examination. I was found unfit to be promoted to the next class because of poor results. At that young age, I thought I was smart. The annual examination results proved quite the contrary. I remember my fellow students jubilant and hurriedly making their way home to tell their parents of their promotion to the next class. I walked over to a park in front of the school, and started to reflect upon what had happened to me. I felt ashamed to have to go home, and tell my parents that I failed in my annual examination. First, I thought that my teachers were unfair to me. Then I thought of many other justifications for what had happened to me. I ultimately came to the realization that I was personally responsible for having failed in the examination. My poor results were due to my own lack of effort. I realized that I had just not prepared for my examination, and I was facing the consequences of that neglect. I knew that I was as intelligent as other students. It is just that I did not make use of my intelligence.

RESULTS ACCOMPLISHED

Within three years of being found unfit to be promoted to the next class, I was elected Prime Minister of my School's Parliament. I was also judged as the best debater in school. And, I was elected President of Delhi Schools Assembly. At the age of 17, I had the honor of presiding at the annual prize distribution function of schools in Delhi. I am just as proud of my academic results. I graduated with good enough academic achievement to get admitted to the Bachelor of Commerce (Honors Course) degree program at Shri Ram College of Commerce in Delhi, the best-known college for commerce education in India. I not only gained admission, I was unanimously elected College Union President at Shri Ram College of Commerce. Also, I won the first prize in an All India Inter-college debate competition. I was awarded Hora Medal by Shri Ram College of Commerce for excellence in student activities. I was elected President of the Delhi University Students Union at the age of 20. And, Delhi University selected me as the leader of its team for an All India Inter-University Group Discussion Competition on All India Radio. Our team won the first prize in that competition. Then I received a scholarship to study in the United States. The scholarship paid for my tuition, room and board, incidentals as well as travel expenses to the United States and back to India.

HOW I ACCOMPLISHED THESE RESULTS?

I adopted and practiced three rules that have paid dividends throughout my life. These rules did not dawn on me suddenly. I acquired them gradually as I thought of ways to get more out of my life. I have practiced these rules in every endeavor.

Here are the three rules that have helped in my life:
- Be Fully Prepared
- Build on Your Strengths
- Believe in Yourself

Rule Number One: Be Fully Prepared

I adopted this rule at the age of 14, and I have practiced it diligently in all activities throughout my life. You cannot go wrong when you have done the needed preparation for any undertaking. If problems arise on the way, you are better prepared to solve those problems. I decided I was always going to do the needed preparation. That meant completing all homework assignments on time, and paying attention to what the teachers were saying in class. I made it a habit to thoroughly prepare for all tasks. It meant knowing what to do and how to do it. Being fully prepared is a very simple and highly effective concept, but most people do not practice it.

To me, being well prepared meant setting out very clearly what I wanted to achieve, having a burning desire to get what I wanted, developing the action steps to get there, establishing completion dates, and then taking the needed steps to accomplish my objective. I did not know at the age of 14 that this was called the goal setting process, but that is exactly what I was trying to do. Being fully prepared also meant finding ways to complete my work in efficient ways. I learned to plan. I would make a list of things to do the next day. This helped me to think about the tasks I had to complete the following day.

I realized early in my life that you need to sow the seeds before you can reap the rewards. Be Fully Prepared is a lesson I have never forgotten. I have followed it rigorously as a student, in my personal life, and in my business career. This is a very simple, but a very dynamic concept. Do your homework, and be well prepared for every situation you are likely to encounter. It is amazing how good you feel when you walk into a situation well prepared, and you can accomplish your goals. Before I go into a meeting, I always write down what I want to cover in the meeting and what I want to accomplish by the end of the meeting. As a result, I have been successful in accomplishing my objectives.

Because I strictly followed the principle of being well prepared, I became successful in my school work. I felt well-adjusted in my environment. This is a lesson that has paid dividends throughout my life. It has become a habit. Whenever I have a task to perform, I ask myself what I need to do to be successful. Then I go about doing the needed preparation. Success is the result one earns from diligent preparation.

I had a very interesting experience back in 1968, just about 3 months after I joined American Express in the United States as a Sales Trainee. I was with a Sales Representative who was training me. We were driving and talking about various people at American Express. I said I was very impressed with our Regional Vice President. That he was a very hard working person. The Sales Representative who was training me turned around and said: "If I was a Regional Vice President, I would work equally hard". I have never forgotten his words. This was an eye opener for me. I realized that a person is expecting results before he is willing to put in the effort. I thought to myself that tremendous things are possible for me if I put in the effort, and then expect results. The Sales Representative who was training me was like someone who sits in front of a fireplace, and says I will put some wood in the fireplace after I get the heat and warmth. Or, like a farmer standing in front of his field saying: "give me a good crop of corn, and then I will plant some seed". We need to sow the seeds before we can reap the rewards.

When I decided in 1997 to get into the executive search business, I realized that I was lacking an essential skill required of a small business owner. I did not know how to use a computer. I borrowed a laptop to see if I could learn to use it. I looked all over the laptop to find a switch that said: "ON". I could not locate such a switch. Finally, I asked my son, Ravi, to show me how to turn on the laptop. It took him just a few seconds to turn on the laptop and its functions. That was my first lesson in learning to use a computer. During the following few weeks, I struggled to learn how to use word processing, how to get on the Internet, how to open e-mails, and how to use search tools on the Internet. It was a very frustrating and time consuming process. Finally, I have learned to make good use of computers and the Internet. I had my own website while I was an executive recruiter, and I continue to make extensive use of computers in my work. Here is a business tool I did not know how to use, and now it is an essential part of my daily life.

Rule Number Two: Build on Your Strengths

As I became successful in achieving what was expected of me by being thoroughly prepared, I looked for ways to accomplish more. I realized that I had great potential, and I was using only a small fraction of it. I realized that I have good qualities that will enable me to move ahead. I became aware that I enjoyed working with people, and I was very good in my interaction with them. I felt that I was well liked by my teachers, fellow students, and friends. I decided to play a leading role in student activities. First I became a class representative to my school's parliament. I took a prominent role in the school parliament activities and became known for my diligence and hard work. Other students supported me and I was successful when I ran for the position of Prime Minister of School Parliament.

My success in student leadership roles continued when I entered college. I joined Shri Ram College of Commerce in 1955. I participated actively in debates and student union programs. I was unanimously elected President of Students Union at Shri Ram College of Commerce in 1957. I received Bachelor of Commerce (Honors Course) degree in 1958, and continued my studies for Master of Commerce at Shri Ram College of Commerce. When I was a student I ran for the office of President of Delhi University Students Union and was elected. The one year I spent as President of Delhi University Students Union taught me more than anything I learned during my college education. It gave me the opportunity to work with students from several colleges affiliated with Delhi University, and it brought me face-to-face with some of the top leaders in India as well as visiting dignitaries from other countries. I urge you to encourage your children to participate in sports and student activities.

Each of us has a different set of strengths. No two individuals are alike. We are all different. It is important to identify our individual strengths and focus on those areas where we can maximize the use of our strengths. I know that I have good communication skills and good interactive skills. I used those skills to play a leading role in student government and debates.

Rule Number Three: Believe in Yourself

There was never a winner in a competition who did not expect to win.

You usually get what you expect. You must have the self-confidence and believe that you will accomplish your goals. I remember that whenever I entered in a debate contest with the firm belief that I was going to win, I did win. And, there were occasions when I had some doubt, and I never won on those occasions. The winner knows the act of winning before it takes place.

While defining your strengths is the starting point, it must be supported by a strong desire to achieve your objectives. By strong desire, I mean a total commitment and a passion for achieving your objectives. One needs to think about the objectives so often that they become embedded in one's subconscious.

Thomas Edison, one of the world's greatest inventors, believed in himself and what he wanted to accomplish. His inventions included the telegraph, phonograph, film projector, and many others including his most famous invention, the light bulb. The light bulb is not just a product of Thomas Edison's imagination; it is a product of his determination. In his pursuit of the light bulb, Thomas Edison completed thousands of experiments. One day, when he had completed 10,000 experiments, a sympathizer walked up to him and said: "Mr. Edison, I am so sorry that you have tried 10,000 times, and you have not been able to invent the electric light bulb". Mr. Edison turned around, and said: "I have not failed 10,000 times. I have found 10,000 ways that won't work". After 12,000 attempts, Thomas Edison developed the first functioning electric light bulb. What would the world be like today if Mr. Edison was less determined?

When good things happen to us, we are always happy. What is needed is to keep a positive attitude and outlook when negative things happen to us. When we come across people at the top of their professions, we often find that they have great attitude. We forget that these people reached the top because of their attitude. Their positive mental attitude is not because of their position. Their high position is because of their positive mental attitude. Success is not a function just of one's intelligence. It results from commitment and determination to accomplish one's goals, and maintaining a positive attitude in the face of adversity.

MY DREAM JOBS

I would like to give you some snapshots from my career to demonstrate how I was able to achieve my dream jobs by using the rules I have described. I would like to focus on two dream jobs in my career. Let me share with you how I got these positions and what they have meant in my life.

The two dream jobs I want to talk about are:
1. President of Delhi University Students Union
2. Sales Executive with American Express Company

President of Delhi University Students Union

At the young age of 20, I was elected President of the Delhi University Students Union. I made full use of the three golden rules I adopted earlier in my life: be fully prepared, make use of your strengths, and believe in yourself. It was a position I envied and thought about when I entered Delhi University as a student. I read newspaper articles about the position and the persons elected to it, and I was awed by its enormous responsibility and prestige. I wondered if I could ever become President of Students Union at Delhi University. While it seemed like an impossible dream, I decided to pursue it. At the age of 18, I decided I was going to turn this dream into a reality. I developed a plan and followed it rigorously for two years. This position was elected by a council of representatives from each of the colleges affiliated with Delhi University. I got myself elected as a representative from my college. Being a member of the council enabled me to interact with other members of the council and build relationships for one year before I wanted to run for election. And, I was fortunate enough to get elected as President of the Students Union in my own college. That gave me some credibility among other members of the council. I participated actively in student debates to develop my public speaking ability and to gain recognition among other students. I accomplished my goal of becoming President of Students Union at Delhi University.

I served as President of Delhi University Students Union during the college year 1958-59. This position had enormous impact on my life during the year in which I served and in the following years.

The position gave me opportunities to meet and exchange ideas with the top leadership in India, including Prime Minister Jawaharlal Nehru, President Rajendra Prasad, and then Vice President Sarvepalli Radhakrishnan who later became President of India. Those meetings are among the most memorable moments of my life. India is very fortunate to have had these three leaders at the top to guide its destiny. They promoted equal opportunity. They focused on removing illiteracy, planning with a long-term vision, and building institutions of higher learning. They sowed the seeds for a democratic and progressive India that exists today. I was most fortunate to have had opportunities to interact with them.

Jawaharlal Nehru served as India's first Prime Minister from the Independence Day in 1947 until he died in 1964. I will always cherish my meeting with Prime Minister Nehru. I met him just a few days before I led an Indian student delegation to Sri Lanka in 1959. We requested the Prime Minister to meet with members of the delegation before we left on our trip to Sri Lanka. He granted our request, and was kind enough to spend almost one hour with us in the conference room of his office in New Delhi. As leader of the delegation, I had the privilege of being seated right next to the Prime Minister. I remember asking him for his advice on acquiring knowledge. He said the way he acquired knowledge was to read books, and grasp them thoroughly. He said he would write a summary of each book he read. And, that enabled him to grasp new concepts and acquire knowledge.

Dr. S. Radhakrishnan was a very eloquent public speaker. He was dynamic, precise, and I loved to listen to every word he spoke. I had the privilege of meeting him at his house along with other representatives from Students Union at Delhi University. I asked him to tell us the secret of effective public speaking. I remember his advice: "develop the ability to stop speaking before the audience wants you to stop". I always keep this advice in mind whenever I have the opportunity to make a presentation.

I remember my meeting with President Rajendra Prasad at Rashtrapati Bhavan (the Presidential House) in New Delhi. He was the first President of independent India. He was kind enough to grant me a one-on-one meeting just before I left for Sri Lanka as the leader of an Indian student delegation. I remember his warmth, humility and graciousness. He made me feel as if I was sitting in the house of a close relative rather than in the house of India's President. I felt so close to President Rajendra Prasad that I sent him a letter inviting him to preside at the Annual Day function of Delhi University Students Union. I was so filled with joy when I received his reply accepting my invitation. I remember that wonderful day in 1959, when I was just 21 years old, sitting on the dais just next to the President of India. What I learned from President Rajendra Prasad was the value of humility and being down to earth.

As President of Delhi University Students Union, I had the opportunity to meet with many leaders in India as well as visiting dignitaries from other countries. I remember a phone call I received in 1959 from Gandhi Smarak Nidhi. They informed me that Dr. Martin Luther King from the United States was in New Delhi, and asked whether I would like to invite him to come to Delhi University and address the students. I arranged Dr. King's lecture, and had the privilege of presiding at that function and introducing Dr. King and his wife to Delhi University students. I had the opportunity of meeting Dr. King once again a couple of years later when he spoke at a meeting in Minneapolis, Minnesota. He remembered his visit to Delhi University, and was gracious enough to ask me to visit him sometime. Unfortunately, I never had another occasion to meet Dr. King. I consider myself very fortunate that I met him on two occasions.

At age 21, I received a scholarship to study in the United States. The scholarship was funded by the Ford Foundation and managed by the United States National Student Association under a program called the "Foreign Student Leadership Project". It was designed to identify students from developing countries with leadership potential and invite them to study in the United States.

I was among a group of 14 students selected from several countries to study at American Universities for one year, and at the same time, take active part in student government and student publications. I was assigned to the University of Minnesota. I stayed in a dormitory and a fraternity house on campus, participated in the day to day activities of the Minnesota Student Association, wrote many articles for The Minnesota Daily, and gave several talks to promote goodwill between India and the United States. Also, I had the opportunity to participate in conferences and seminars throughout the U. S. It was a great experience to interact with American students, and to share ideas and experiences with student leaders from several countries who were participating in this foreign student leadership project.

While I was studying at the University of Minnesota, I received an invitation to join a group called "Ambassadors for Friendship".

This group was put together by Harry and Kathleen Morgan, a charming couple, who wanted to promote a better understanding of foreign cultures among Americans, and at the same time, give some of the foreign students a better idea of how the Americans live. Harry and Kathy would select three to four foreign students each year during the summer college break to travel with them in a car for about four weeks and interact with people from various walks of life. I was fortunate enough to be selected for this program in the summer of 1960. Harry Morgan got American Motors to donate a new Rambler station wagon for this trip and he made a lot of personal effort to raise the needed funds to finance the trip. There were five of us who made the trip: Harry and Kathleen Morgan, Kofi Annan from Ghana, Nassar Mazaheri from Iran, and Narinder Mehta from India. We started from St. Paul, Minnesota and went all the way to California. We got a terrific overview of life in various communities. We met with religious groups, attended political events, and gave talks at many gatherings in several cities. A highlight of this trip was a meeting with President Harry S. Truman at his library in Independence, Missouri. He was kind enough to spend one hour with us and freely answered all the questions we put to him. We also met with President Lyndon B. Johnson at a picnic in Oklahoma City (he was running for President of the United States at that time). I will never forget his looking straight in my eyes, with his hand firmly placed on my shoulder, and telling me how much he loved India and its people.

After that wonderful summer traveling in many parts of the United States, I returned to the University of Minnesota. I enjoyed the student life in Minneapolis. After living in a dormitory for three months, I moved into Tau Kappa Epsilon, a fraternity house. I enjoyed my interaction with other members of the fraternity, and they were kind enough to ask me to serve as a Residence Counselor in the fraternity. That was an honor and a great experience. I greatly enjoyed my education and activities in Minnesota. I was granted Master of Arts degree in Industrial Relations by the University of Minnesota in December 1961.

As I was completing my studies at the University of Minnesota, I accepted an offer from the National Council of University Students of India to join them as Executive Secretary upon my return to India. That was a great opportunity to build the national student organization in India by working with student leaders from universities all over the country. It enabled me to interact with student leaders from other countries as well, and gave me the privilege of serving as a Co-Chairman of the International Student Conference held in 1962 at the campus of Laval University in Canada. Working with the national student organization in India was a lot of fun, but this job was not a path to a career. I felt the urge to find a job in business so that I could start building my career. I started looking at newspaper ads for job vacancies, and began the process of applying for jobs to find a suitable opportunity in the Indian industry.

My first job in industry was with the All India Management Association in New Delhi starting in January 1963. I saw a newspaper advertisement for a job that seemed suited to my background and qualifications. I applied, got an interview, and a job offer. I started as a Program Officer, and within two years, I was promoted to Program Director with full responsibility for the planning and administration of all training and management development programs throughout India. I conducted seminars on planning and implementing management development in several cities. Also, I had the good fortune to have day to day interaction with senior managers of many private and public sector companies. My experiences with the All India Management Association enabled me to learn about different companies and functional areas in Indian industry. After four years with the All India Management Association, I decided in 1967 to move to the United States. I felt that I had the education and experience to build a wonderful career in the United States.

Sales Executive with American Express Company

My first dream job in the United States was with American Express Company where I spent 17 years working in positions of increasingly higher responsibility in several locations.

I started as a Sales Trainee in Chicago with the Money Order Division of American Express. Within the first 4 years, I became District Sales Manager in Detroit, Regional Sales Manager for Michigan, Ohio, and Kentucky, and then Regional Vice President of Sales for the Eastern Region of the United States. Subsequently, I became National Sales Director of the American Express Gold Card and Vice President, Sales of the American Express Corporate Card. I was then elected as a Senior Vice President of Shearson/American Express.

My pursuit of a sales position with American Express is a good illustration of how your life and career are shaped when you follow your dreams.

Let me share my story with you. I decided when I was 29 years old to make my home in the United States. I had acquired a Master of Arts degree from the University of Minnesota during a previous stay in the United States. I had management experience of four years with the All India Management Association. I thought it would be easy for me to find a good job. I prepared a resume listing my education, experiences, and accomplishments. I sent many resumes during the first month, many more the second month, and a lot more during the third month. As I look back upon my job search experience, I realize the many mistakes I made in my job search. I now urge others to avoid the mistakes I made such as mass distribution of resumes. It appeared that the Human Resources Departments of the companies I approached were using a standard response letter. I kept getting the response that basically said: "You have a good background and qualifications, but we do not have an opportunity that will be a good match." After looking for a suitable position for three months, I took a job in a warehouse doing manual work. My job title in the warehouse was "Order Filler". My job duties were to go around the warehouse with a shopping cart and fill it with the merchandise ordered by commercial customers. It was not very exciting work, but it helped to pay the rent and food expenses. I kept sending my resume to more and more companies.

When I was in the 7th month of looking for a professional opportunity, I saw an ad from American Express looking for a Sales Representative in Minneapolis, Minnesota. I sent my resume, and I was delighted when I got a call for interview. The interview was scheduled at a Holiday Inn in downtown Minneapolis. It was a couple of miles from my apartment, but I decided to walk the distance to save on expenses. The road was damp and my shoes were wet when I reached the Holiday Inn.

I arrived for the interview, and was very impressed by the person conducting the interview. His name is John Kurowski. He had charisma, warmth, and excellent communications ability. I said to myself: "Here is a person I would really like to work for. That will be a great way to build my career in the

United States". I had a good interview, and I was advised by John Kurowski that another manager will conduct a second interview. I expressed my enthusiasm and interest in the opportunity. He said he will ask his Regional Sales Manager to do a second interview. I had a second interview, and that seemed to go well. I thought that a job offer was going to come from American Express, and I eagerly waited for that call. On the third day after my interview, I got a call from the Regional Sales Manager. He said they have found an experienced Sales Representative in Minneapolis, and American Express cannot offer me a job. I was crushed. I thought I had the job I really wanted, and they turned me down.

I sat down that day and spent several hours thinking about the contributions I could make to American Express, and why they should hire me. The following day I called John Kurowski, Regional Vice President of American Express; the person who conducted the first interview. I expressed to him the reasons why I was a good match for American Express, and why the company should hire me. He said he will call back. The following day he called, and said that while the company did not have a Sales Representative position open, they were willing to create a sales trainee position for me in Chicago. I was delighted, and I accepted the offer. That was the start of a wonderful career with American Express.

I mention this experience to you because it points out what is possible when you are determined, make the needed preparation, and pursue what you desire. Here is something I desired strongly and to which I dedicated myself. I committed my time and resources to put together a list of reasons why I was a good match for a sales position with American Express. I organized my reasons, I practiced what I was going to say, and then I picked up the courage to make a phone call to a senior executive at American Express. That effort had a dramatic impact on my life. I feel wonderful to this day for that extra effort, and I have certainly reaped the rewards. It is necessary to make the extra effort to differentiate yourself from other candidates. When you are interviewing for the job you really desire, make that extra effort, and I believe you will be rewarded with success.

There was another benefit to me more meaningful than all the professional satisfaction I had from working for American Express.

John Kurowski, who created the sales trainee position for me at American Express, and I became good friends. He was kind enough to invite me to spend many wonderful evenings with him and his wife at their home in Chicago. I remember a telephone call he made to me in October 1970 when his third son was born. He called to ask if I would be willing to become his third son's Godfather. I said: "I will be honored". Then he asked another question that I will never forget. He asked if he could give my middle name "Kumar" as the middle name for his newly born son. There is today a young man at the age of 50 in Denver, Colorado named Steven Kumar Kurowski. I am very proud of him.

My association with American Express was a critical time in my career. My work history at American Express laid the ground work for my professional success. As I reflect upon what enabled me to succeed at American Express, it becomes clear that it was due to the application of the three golden rules I learned in high school: Be Fully Prepared; Build on Your Strengths; and Believe in Yourself.

Career after American Express

I left American Express after 17 wonderful years and joined Capital Credit Corporation as Senior Vice President

– Marketing and Sales and a member of the Board of Directors. The decision to leave American Express was the toughest career decision of my life. I spent several days thinking about it before I submitted my letter of resignation. I decided ultimately to leave American Express because of my desire to have a bigger role in a smaller company. I worked for Capital Credit Corporation for 9 years. Then I joined Outsourcing Solutions Inc. and served as Senior Vice President of International Marketing. I worked for Outsourcing Solutions for 4 years, and then decided to start my own company.

I founded an executive search firm in 1997 and served as its President for ten years. My firm became a leading provider of executive search services to the financial services industry. My clients included banks, credit card issuers, and large call centers. I specialized in finding executive talent for middle level and senior management positions. I filled positions throughout the United States. I was also able to place Americans for management positions in other countries. As an executive recruiter, I reviewed thousands of resumes and interviewed hundreds of candidates. I had daily interaction with hiring managers at some of the largest employers. My experiences in recruiting have given me a good understanding of what the employers look for in making hiring decisions, and how the candidates can position themselves to effectively demonstrate their talents and suitability for available openings. The job as an executive recruiter was the best job I ever had.

I attribute most of what I have been able to accomplish in my life to my response to the stunning setback I received when I was just 14 years old. My response was to accept full responsibility for my failure in the school examination, and then develop and follow a plan to prevent that from happening again. It was that response at the age of 14 that started the engine within me that has propelled me throughout my life. Whenever you are confronted with a major setback, ask yourself the question: What was my responsibility for that outcome? What I need to do to prevent it from happening again? If you rigorously follow the direction your response will provide, I have no doubt you will achieve great success in your career.

A major setback is often the test of your character

How you deal with a major setback can enhance your capabilities and your confidence. When you choose to learn from your mistakes, you rebound from failure and move towards achievement. Success comes from learning the lessons taught by failure. You must accept responsibility for why you failed, and determine how you are going to avoid those mistakes in the future. Your response to a failure determines whether it is going to destroy you or make you stronger and more successful in the future.

The direction I received from within to become successful was to focus on the three principles: Be Fully Prepared; Build on Your Strengths; and Believe in Yourself. I have followed these principles diligently, and that has helped me to accomplish the goals I set for myself. The direction you receive from your soul searching may lead you to the same principles or some other principles that will drive you to success. Once you have formulated your principles, please remember that just the knowledge of those principles is not enough. It is the application of the principles you have adopted for your success that will help you achieve what you desire. To reap the rewards, you must apply your principles in your daily life.

ACKNOWLEDGEMENTS

To author a book requires the help of many people. This book would not have come about without the support of many friends and family members. I want to single out a few individuals for their exceptional contributions.

Connie Wanberg has amazed me with her generosity. She is a Professor and Industrial Relations Faculty Excellence Chair in the Work and Organizations Department at the Carlson School of Management, University of Minnesota. She read the manuscript and devoted much time and effort to ensure this book would be a good resource for finding jobs and building successful careers. She found my mistakes, made corrections, and suggested many ways to improve the content. She has certainly made this book more valuable.

Dr. Doris Helge is a great supporter. She has been recommending my books to her clients for many years. She is a career coach and has authored "Joy on the Job" and other bestsellers. She reviewed the manuscript and has submitted a testimonial that appears on the back cover.

Joe Barsi helped me with my last book and was good enough to review this book's manuscript. He made many valuable suggestions for changes and additions. He has an impressive record of accomplishments and now serves as President at California Giant Berry Farms.

Rochelle Sollish, Founder/President at the Marketing Garage in Los Angeles reviewed the manuscript and made many suggestions to improve the content and its presentation. She has a keen marketing sense and helped to improve this book.

Charlie Galloway reviewed an early draft of the book. He came up with many ideas to improve the content and suggested some additions. It is great to have such a talented friend. I have known Charlie since we worked together at American Express.

Sudhir Bansal is a perfectionist and does not miss a mistake. He devoted a lot of time and effort to review the book's manuscript and made excellent suggestions. We have been friends for many years. We both used to work in New York City and got together for lunch from time to time.

R. Balachandran read the manuscript from start to finish and then went back and checked each chapter to make sure that the content would be useful for the readers. He suggested some changes and many of those changes are included in the book.

Howard Knauer knows the jobs market very well. He has managed hundreds of employees for many large banks and other companies. He was good enough to review the manuscript to make sure that the book's content will be useful for the readers.

Russ Schoper went through the manuscript and made many helpful suggestions to improve the quality of presentation. Russ and I were colleagues at American Express. He is now President of Business Development International.

John Kurowski is a person who has had a profound impact on my career as well as personal life. We met when he was a Regional Vice President with American Express Company and hired me as a sales trainee. We have been friends ever since. He is the Godfather of my son, Ravi Kurowski Mehta, and I am the proud Godfather of his son, Steven Kumar Kurowski. I look for John's help and support on many projects.

Steve Kurowski reviewed the manuscript and suggested some additional information to make the book more useful for the readers.

My son, Ravi Mehta, read the manuscript and made many valuable suggestions to improve the content. He loves books and has given me some great books to read. He holds an MBA from the MIT Sloan School of Management. He is married to Tiffany Christian Mehta, and I am blessed to have two wonderful granddaughters named Arden and Vivien.

My brother, Patanjali Mehta, has saved and organized my records for several years. He is always able to produce the information I need, no matter how old. Some of the content of this book is due to his excellent record keeping.

Above all, I want to thank my wife, Sampath. She is the most caring person, not just for me, but for everyone around. She has been a great source of encouragement. She is an Anesthesiologist and has served many institutions including the Montefiore Medical Center in New York. I am grateful for her unwavering support.

I am very fortunate that so many experts were good enough to give their time to improve this book's content and accuracy. I may still have managed to sneak in some mistakes while they were not looking. For that, I take full responsibility.

Thank you for reading my book. I want to wish you a very successful and happy career!

INDEX

ABOUT THE AUTHOR

Narinder Mehta was President of an executive search firm for ten years. Prior to that, he worked in the financial services industry. He served as a Senior Vice President at several companies including Shearson/American Express, Capital Credit Corporation, and Outsourcing Solutions Inc. He was National Sales Director of the American Express Gold Card program and served as Vice President of Sales for the American Express Corporate Card. He had the honor of serving as a National Vice President of the Muscular Dystrophy Association for two terms. He is the author of three previous books on job search and career development. He has spoken on goals accomplishment and personal development to audiences in many countries. He received his Master of Arts degree in Industrial Relations from the University of Minnesota and Bachelor of Commerce (Honors Course) degree from the University of Delhi. He lives in Dover, Massachusetts, with his wife, Sampath.

E-mail: jobsbook1@aol.com
LinkedIn: www.linkedin.com/in/NarinderMehta
Twitter: http://twitter.com/NarinderM

Made in the USA
Middletown, DE
17 August 2021

45574967R00139